ERASING ISRAEL

SEVEN DEADLY LIES THAT REWRITE GOD'S PROMISES AND FUEL FALSE PROPHECY.

Destiny Image Books by Alan Didio

Erasing Israel: Seven Deadly Lies That Rewrite God's Promises and Fuel False Prophecy

They Lied to You About Prosperity: The Shocking Truth About God's Plan for Wealth and Abundance

They Lied to You About the Rapture: How to Prepare for What's Coming

Summoning the Demon: AI, Aliens, and the Antichrist

Armed for Victory: Prayer Strategies That Unlock the End-Time Armory of God

ERASING ISRAEL

SEVEN DEADLY LIES THAT REWRITE GOD'S PROMISES AND FUEL FALSE PROPHECY.

ALAN DIDIO

 All emphasis within Scripture quotations is the author's own. Take note that the name satan and related names are not capitalized. We choose not to acknowledge him, even to the point of violating grammatical rules.

DESTINY IMAGE® PUBLISHERS, INC.
P.O. Box 310, Shippensburg, PA 17257-0310
"Publishing cutting-edge prophetic resources to supernaturally empower the body of Christ"

This book and all other Destiny Image and Destiny Image Fiction books are available at Christian bookstores and distributors worldwide.

For more information on foreign distributors, call 717-532-3040.
Reach us on the Internet: www.destinyimage.com.

ISBN 13 TP: 979-8-8815-1008-4
ISBN 13 eBook: 979-8-8815-1009-1

For Worldwide Distribution, Printed in the U.S.A.
1 2 3 4 5 6 7 8 / 30 29 28 27 26

CONTENTS

INTRODUCTION

There is a dangerous deception filtering into the theology of the modern Church and spreading into the populace at large. It is a deception so alarming and so demoralizing that it stands to rock the Church to the very core of its belief system.

It is a doctrine so controversial that the theological pundits of our day have grabbed hold of it and caused it to spread like wildfire through their social media circles.

Controversy means an increase in viewers, and an increase in viewers means more likes and shares, and more likes and shares lead to more money coming in from the purchase of sponsored products. Controversy can turn a culture of worship into a culture of commerce and we know how Jesus dealt with that!

It is also a philosophy so disturbing that it is having an undue effect on current geopolitics. Where once we considered antisemitism—despising of Jews and the desire to stamp out their culture—to be a thing of the past, yet this false ideology is once again fueling and fanning the flames of hatred.

I am referring to the insidious and odious madness of *replacement theology*. This doctrinal issue, also referred to as *supersessionism,* is the belief that the Church has replaced Israel. It purports that the Jewish people and the nation of Israel have been replaced by the Church.

But the Bible is clear: the Church has *not* replaced Israel! In this book, I refute the lie that the nation of Israel is at odds with the truth of the Word of God; and I show you why that lie, and the truth, matter to us.

If God would break His covenant with Israel and cut them off from the blessings He has promised them from antiquity, where does that leave you and me? Can we still trust God to keep the promises He has made to *us?* Is our salvation certain? Is a home in Heaven truly on the horizon?

Of what benefit is a covenant if it can simply be erased and its promises given to another? If we cannot trust in and rely on the promises we see in the Word of God, Christianity will implode as its former adherents slink away in a humiliated haze!

My purpose in this book is to put an end to this madness and reveal it for what it truly is—an adulteration of the Holy Scriptures. It is time to stop the lie. When truth is known, a lie will have no power—no power to bring harm to God's chosen people. It will no longer have the power to rob you of your faith.

No longer will this false theology have the power to turn people away from the God who has both *chosen* and *promised* to love them with an *eternal* love, through an *everlasting* covenant. The Word of God is most certainly true—you will know the truth, and the truth will set you free!

Bishop Alan Didio Charlotte, North Carolina

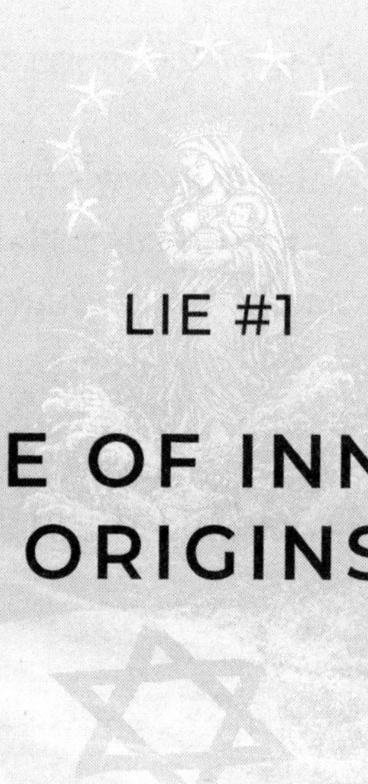

LIE #1

THE LIE OF INNOCENT ORIGINS

Get ready to discover some history your pastor never taught you. In considering this doctrinal issue, the first question that comes to mind is this: *What does the concept of replacement theology mean, and where and how did such a concept begin?*

I am reluctant to call this phenomenon *replacement theology*. I believe that does a disservice to the legitimate branches of theology. However, since replacement theology is how it is generally known, I will use that terminology.

Additionally, it has been called *supersessionism*. This term, created from the root word *supersede*, helps explain the concept. Let's break it down: to supersede means that one thing takes the place of another. The literal meaning, then, of supersessionism is the belief that one thing has been superseded, or replaced, by another—in this case, the nation of Israel has been replaced by the Church.

There are different flavors of this doctrine, and some will no doubt take issue with the definition I am including here, but the essential facts remain the same. Replacement theology is the belief that the Church has replaced both the nation of Israel and the Jewish people. It is the belief that the promises God gave to Israel now belong to the Church.

Some theologians may prefer to use the terms *fulfillment theology* or *covenant theology*, but the result is the same. This doctrine effectively strips Israel of the blessings and promises given by God and transfers them to the Church. Replacement theology claims that Israel's status as God's chosen people has been taken away and given to the Church.

Dispensationalism: The Dual Covenant View

Supersessionism is in contrast to dispensationalism, which is a literal, dual covenant view of Israel and the Church.

Dispensationalism is simply dividing Bible history into certain time periods. A *dispensation* refers to a specific period of time in Bible history. For example, the time period from the inception of the early Church until now is often referred to as the dispensation, or time, of the Church. Some call it the time of the Gentiles. The fact that one dispensation is in progress does not negate another.

A *dual covenant view* means that the covenant of God with Israel *and* the covenant of God with the Church are both equally valid. Israel has a covenant with God; the Church has a covenant with God. They are not mutually exclusive. Dispensationalism allows both covenants to coexist.

Israel was given the law that we now refer to as part of the Old Covenant (dependence on a system of sacrifices). The Church is now governed by the New Covenant (faith in the redemptive work of Christ).

Of course, we understand that certain moral and ethical aspects of the Old Covenant, such as the prohibition against murder, overlap with the New Covenant. The requirements for human behavior under the New Covenant, however, exceed that of the Old Covenant, as Jesus described in Matthew 5 in the passage referred to as the Sermon on the Mount.

This deserves some additional consideration. Under the Old Covenant, worshipers were required to obey the law as given to Moses by God at Mount Sinai. It was impossible for them to obey the law perfectly, so God instituted a sacrificial system that enabled their trespasses to be covered, most often by the blood of a sacrificial animal.

Under the New Covenant, believers are also required to obey the law—but not the law of Moses. The law of the New Covenant is the *law of love*, demonstrated to perfection by the life of the Lord Jesus Christ.

We cannot obey this law any more than a worshiper under the Old Covenant could obey the law of Moses. One of the greatest advantages of the New Covenant is that when we transgress the law of love, we don't have to bring an animal to a priest. The sacrifice that redeems us from sin has already been provided as a result of Christ's sacrifice on the Cross. We access that redemption, or forgiveness, by repentance. The price has already been paid.

What we must do is trust in Jesus Christ as Savior instead of attempting to fulfill the requirements of the law of Moses. Believing in Jesus presents its own set of challenges, but it is far easier than trying to fulfill all the requirements of the law!

However, I must say this very clearly: believing in Jesus and participating in a better covenant established upon better promises does not cause us to replace the Jewish people or the nation of Israel in God's plan for humanity, for the earth, or for the ages. To say that it does strays far from the bounds of the Word of God or His purposes.

Not only that, but replacement theology also inevitably leads to bigger problems that are even today still intruding on the world's stage. Antisemitism is one of those problems.

Antisemitism

It will not surprise you to know that the dismissive attitude of one people group toward another is nothing new. In fact, it has been part of the human condition since the separation of nations at the tower of Babel (see Genesis 11:1-9). I believe it is instructive to see how God's people dealt with other people groups from the beginning of the church age.

One of the first indications of this is in Acts 10. Cornelius was a Roman soldier; Peter was an apostle of the Lord. Both of these men received divine revelation that led to the Gentiles receiving the gospel and becoming part of the Church. The reason this is so significant is that up to that time, there were serious questions among believers about whether the heathen Gentiles could even be saved.

This was confirmed by the attitude of those who accompanied Peter. The Bible says in Acts 10:45 that they were *"astonished"* that the Holy Spirit fell on the Gentiles. Other translations use the terms *surprised, amazed,* and *astounded.* These words represent a very strong feeling—they would not have had that attitude if they had expected Gentiles to be included in God's plan from the beginning.

I find it fascinating that today the script has flipped, so to speak. Now, instead of Jewish believers doubting that the Gentiles could be saved, we see believers who adhere to replacement theology discounting and even denying the importance or relevance of Jews in God's plan.

Several historical events played into the development of this mindset.

The Council of Elvira: This attitude of considering Jews or interactions with Jews to be unacceptable has its historical roots in the Council of Elvira that was convened in AD 305. This council was a group of Spanish church leaders who met to attempt to give direction and discipline to growing church communities of the day.

The result was 81 disciplinary canons, or church laws, which sought to direct proper Christian behavior. One of the canons forbade Christians to marry Jews. Others went even further and forbade eating meals with Jews or having certain other forms of interaction with them that had apparently become customary.

Regardless of the intention of these laws, the effect was to emphasize separation from other groups. The purpose of this was undoubtedly, at least in part, to maintain the distinctiveness of Christian communities. However, another effect of these edicts was the "othering" of another people group.

Separation often means more than distinction. It almost inevitably means that the people who are maintaining separation develop an attitude of superiority over others. This has devastating consequences, as history attests. This is not something as simple as believing that your home team is better than the visiting team. This attitude can very easily lead to extremes in belief and behavior toward others, either as individuals or entire people groups.

The Council of Nicaea: A few years later, the Christian council of Nicaea was convened to discuss the doctrine of the deity of Christ and other church matters, including the date of Easter. Perhaps the most familiar result of this council was the development of the Nicene Creed—a statement of faith issued by the Council of Nicaea that is still recited in certain churches today.

The council did circulate a letter addressing the need to separate the Christian Easter from the Jewish Passover. The letter claimed that the Jews had made a mistake in their reckoning of the dates for Passover, and urged Christians not to adopt these dates. Because of this letter, some accused the council of dismissing the Jews as repulsive or offensive, but this was untrue.

Although this language could be considered less than inflammatory, it was used later as an example of how Christians and Jews should remain separate. In addition, it carried the weight of Emperor Constantine's name.

The Edict of Milan: The attitude of separation gained momentum during the 4th century. A significant shift came because of the Edict of Milan in AD 313. This statement was a political agreement between Constantine, the emperor of the western half of the Roman empire, and Licinius, the ruler of the eastern half.

Among other things, it granted complete religious freedom to all citizens, not only to Christians. It also ended state-sponsored persecution of Christians, restored confiscated Christian property, including churches and meeting places, and affirmed freedom of conscience, allowing individuals to worship any deity they chose.

You can imagine what a relief this was to Christians who had been suffering the threat of persecution for many years under previous Roman regimes. What this also meant was that Christians no longer had to rely on the Jewish umbrella, so to speak, that had allowed them to grow without the constant threat of Roman restrictions.

In the early days of Christianity, Judaism had long been a recognized religion in the empire. Christianity was not. Therefore, as long as Rome regarded Christians as just another sect of Judaism, it would for the most part leave the Christians alone.

When Rome came to the point where it recognized that Christianity was not part of Judaism, the period of the most severe and prolonged persecutions of Christians began. That persecution was cut short by the Edict of Milan. It also removed the Christians' reliance on Judaism to allow it to flourish.

The Edict of Thessalonica: What happened in the mid- to late 4th century caused anti-Jewish sentiment to develop even among Christian communities. One factor that fueled this was when Emperor Theodosius I declared Christianity to be the official religion of Rome. This led to the sentiment that Judaism was spiritually obsolete and that the Jews didn't understand their own scriptures.

Proponents of this theory often used what they pointed out as Jewish errors to promote the truth of what they were saying. This has been a debate tactic since antiquity: "They believe *x*, but in contrast to their extreme, unreasonable, and ultimately insupportable opinion, we believe *y*." Watch for this mentality the next time you view a political debate!

Emperor Theodosius I issued the Edict of Thessalonica in AD 380. This was the law that essentially made Christianity the official religion of the Roman Empire. Rather than being a relatively small and poor persecuted minority, Christianity now had the backing of the weight of the empire. It now became fashionable, and even preferable, to be considered a Christian. As you can imagine, not everyone who claimed to be a Christian really was one. (Some things never change.)

The other side of this story is that along with the ascendancy of Christianity, restrictions came to Judaism. These included less approvals for synagogue construction, penalties for Jews who tried to convert Christians, and preference for Christian testimony in legal matters.

Inequality between Christians and Jews was now institutionalized, and anti-Jewish hostility was legitimized. The idea that the Church had replaced Israel became more systematic. It led to more polemic preaching against Jews and Judaism. This created a theological framework that justified social and legal marginalization of Jews in the Roman Empire.

The Paradox: These developments created a curious and even dangerous paradox. On one hand, the 4th-century Church preached against Jews and Judaism. They acted out their beliefs in some instances by going as far as to attack synagogues. At the same time, they continued to use the Jewish scriptures as their Bible, they acknowledged Jesus as Jewish, and they recognized that they were the beneficiaries of Jewish history and heritage. This cognitive dissonance has not diminished in the centuries since then.

The Medieval and Modern Periods

This point of view continued to grow during the subsequent medieval period and progressed along these lines. First, there were mobs who killed Jews in certain cities in Europe associated with the beginning of the Crusades. Then, Christians and others falsely accused Jews of certain aspects of ritual sacrifice that are shocking and disturbing—among them child sacrifice. How these accusations reached the threshold of credibility is unknown, but it resulted in Jews being ostracized, persecuted, and even expelled from some regions or countries.

In some places, Jews were required to identify themselves by distinctive clothing or badges that distinguished themselves to others as Jews. Christian teaching also increasingly blamed Jews for the death of Jesus and for the persecution of early Christians. As these points of view became more widespread, violence against Jews became easier to justify.

Martin Luther: Perhaps the best-known proponent of these ideas was Martin Luther, the reformer whose ideas sparked an upheaval that continues to this day. Regarding his attitude toward Jews, Luther's life and ministry can be divided into three periods.

The first involves a tone of hope that the Jews would be converted to Christianity. The second involves disappointment, and later anger that they had not turned to Christ. The third was a period of virulent and even violent rhetoric against the Jews and all that they represented. How violent? In his *On the Jews and Their Lies*, published in 1543, Luther:

- Calls for burning synagogues
- Advocates destroying Jewish homes
- Urges confiscation of Jewish books

- Calls for rabbis to be forbidden to teach
- Recommends expulsion if Jews refuse conversion

Let me share with you some of the rhetoric he used against the Jews. It may be difficult to read, especially in terms of the way many think of Luther today. We are familiar with Martin Luther's desire for reform within the Church. He wanted to engage in a thought-provoking conversation when he affixed his 95 theses to the door of the Castle Church in Wittenberg on October 31, 1517.

Because of this, we tend to view him as a statesman, the champion of religious reform. Rose-colored glasses? You decide. What we don't often hear are his violent feelings against the Jews.

Let me share a few of his comments with you from his treatise titled *On the Jews and Their Lies*:

1. Stupid Fools, thieves and robbers, the great vermin of humanity....[1]
2. Judaism is the spiritual-biological poisoning of our race.[2]
3. My advice, as I said earlier, is: First, that their synagogues be burned down, and that all who are able toss in sulfur and pitch; it would be good if someone could also throw in some hellfire...we have now given them their due reward.[3]

4. Second, that all their books—their prayer books, their Talmudic writings, also the entire Bible—be taken from them.... Third, that they be forbidden on pain of death to praise God, to give thanks, to pray.... Fourth, that they be forbidden to utter the name of God within our hearing.... He who hears this name from a Jew must inform the authorities, or else throw sow dung at him when he sees him and chase him away. And may no one be merciful and kind in this regard.[4]
5. I advise that their houses also be razed and destroyed.[5]
6. It is impossible to convert the devil and his own, nor are we commanded to attempt this.[6]
7. Perhaps, one of the merciful Saints among us Christians may think I am behaving too crude and disdainfully against the poor, miserable Jews in that I deal with them so insulting. But, good God, I am much too mild in insulting such devils.[7]

Martin Luther was most certainly a product of his culture. By the time he died in 1546, he was a confirmed antisemite. It seemed that no amount of thoughtful reasoning could cause him to adjust or temper his point of view.

This points out another principle that I need to mention: replacement theology is only a precursor to full-blown antisemitism. As evidence of this, Luther's polemics against the Jews would become very useful to a certain group nearly 500 years later.

While the roots of replacement theology can be traced to antiquity, the foul fruit of this doctrine is ripening in the minds of believers and others even now. Rather than being discredited and discarded, it seems to be gaining momentum even in our so-called enlightened age. I think it is instructive to see what other world leaders have said about not just this doctrine, but about Jews in general in the past century.

Adolf Hitler: The most well-known of these, of course, is undoubtedly Adolf Hitler. From the time of his rise to power in Germany in 1933 until his death in 1945, he was the primary force behind antisemitism in the world. His rhetoric, actions, and policies resulted in the premeditated and systematic death of six million Jews—a disaster known as the Holocaust. Hitler went as far as to cite Christian leaders of past generations (including Martin Luther) to claim that he was doing the will of God by exterminating Jews. The following is one of the statements Hitler made concerning the Jews:

> In 1924 at a Christian gathering in Berlin, Hitler spoke to thousands and received a standing ovation when he made the following proclamation: "I believe that today I am acting in accordance with the will of Almighty

> God as I announce the most important work that Christians could undertake, and that is to be against the Jews and get rid of them once and for all."[8]

It's often said that the churches were silent during the Holocaust in Europe—the sad truth is that many of them were supporting it.

Joseph Stalin: During Joseph Stalin's reign as the head of the Soviet Union, his propaganda machine portrayed Jews, especially Jewish intellectuals, as enemies of the Soviet state. During this period, Jews were referred to as rootless cosmopolitans, who were disloyal or aligned with foreign powers. As you can imagine, this produced widespread antisemitism in the Soviet Union. This program of antisemitism also spilled over into Soviet satellite states, especially in Eastern Europe.

The United States: The United States has not been immune to this antisemitic influence. Fringe political figures, captains of industry, and popular personalities alike have promoted conspiracy theories about Jews controlling the media or finance. They also either implied or said outright that Jews were disloyal and could not be trusted.

The Middle East: We cannot forget the usual suspects—certain Middle Eastern leaders who either used antisemitism to whip up sentiment against Israel or made it a cornerstone of their domestic and foreign policies.

Europe: Even certain far-right leaders in Europe have advocated for either minimizing or denying the Holocaust, claimed that Jews controlled or manipulated global politics or immigration, and portrayed Jews as incompatible with national identity.

Current Day: All of these points are being echoed in current statements from thought leaders, media influencers, and others in entertainment, finance, education, and business. This has three main themes, in addition to (but arising from) replacement theology. They are:

- Boycott, Divestment, and Sanctions (BDS) against Israel
- Continued Holocaust denial, despite overwhelming evidence and eyewitness testimony of the reality and brutality of this horrific chapter in human history
- Reflexively taking a position against or promoting conspiracy theories about Israel or the Jews in every conflict, controversy, or argument

The Infallible Source of Truth

We have looked at what the religious and political thought leaders of their day have said, written, or in some way disseminated and promoted about replacement theology.

However, in the interest of infallible truth, there is one more Source we need to consider: *What does the Bible say about Israel and the concept of replacement theology?*

I plan to explore this subject much more thoroughly in the following chapters. But in short, the Bible does not say anything about specific about replacement theology, but it does have much to say about the nation of Israel and the Jewish people.

God's concern for Israel and the Jews is neither fleeting nor transitory—it is permanent and abiding. Here is one sample from Isaiah 49:14-18:

> But Zion said, The Lord hath forsaken me, and my Lord hath forgotten me. Can a woman forget her sucking child, that she should not have compassion on the son of her womb? yea, they may forget, yet will I not forget thee. Behold, I have graven thee upon the palms of my hands; thy walls are continually before me.
>
> Thy children shall make haste; thy destroyers and they that made thee waste shall go forth of thee. Lift up thine eyes round about, and behold: all these gather themselves together, and come to thee. As I live, saith the Lord, thou shalt surely clothe thee with them all, as with an ornament, and bind them on thee, as a bride doeth.

This passage, and many similar ones, have no reference to the Church. They have always referred to the nation of Israel and her people, the Jews. This section of Isaiah deals with the future restoration of Israel—not the nation we see now in the Middle East, but Israel as it will be in the days to come.

Before that day can come, though, we need to understand the basis of God's dealings with His people Israel. Where did they originate? What was their connection to the Most High God? What were they promised; how were they blessed?

Now you won't be fooled by the lie of innocent origins because you know how replacement theology is connected with antisemitism.

In the next chapter, we will explore the biblical basis for the covenant God made with Israel. This is a long-standing covenant. It is a covenant whose connection to the Church is one of types and shadows, a representation of things to come, but not a replacement for them.

Notes

1 Martin Luther, *On the Jews and Their Lies* (1543), quoted in "Martin Luther: The Jews and Their Lies," Bible Topics; http://www.bibletopics.com/biblestudy/117.htm.

2 Ibid.

3 Ibid.

4 Ibid.

5 Ibid.

6 Ibid.

7 Ibid.

8 Phyllis Petty, "Christian Hatred and Persecution of the Jews," https://tedhayes.us/TedHayes-site-on-computer/Atone_christian_hatred_and_persecution.htm.

LIE #2

THE LIE OF THE CANCELED PROMISE

The meeting appeared to be random, but it was by no means a result of chance. How could chance account for such an encounter? The man had never heard of such a thing before. In all his experience, and in all the stories and legends he had heard from his family members and acquaintances, nothing could have prepared him for what he was facing now.

He was familiar with the rituals and routines of worshiping his family's gods. He was married, and looked forward to having children of his own and making a life that continued the traditions he had known in his home city.

In an instant, everything had changed. A God he did not know existed—and had never heard of before—had spoken to him. This God had given him a task to fulfill. He had never felt like he felt now. He could not deny the reality of the experience, and he had a defined sense of purpose. He did not know how he would explain it to his family—or to his wife.

He would have to leave his home and all that was familiar to him and embark on a long, arduous, and possibly dangerous journey—following a voice he had never before heard to a land he had never before seen.

It was a scenario filled with peril, but he knew that it was real, and he knew that it was right. To delay would be to disobey. He began making preparations immediately.

I may have taken some liberties with this story, but it is shrouded in antiquity. Perhaps my imagination is no less credible than anyone else's. Here is how the Bible describes what happened, from Genesis 12:1-3:

> Now the Lord had said unto Abram, Get thee out of thy country, and from thy kindred, and from thy father's house, unto a land that I will shew thee: And I

> will make of thee a great nation, and I will bless thee, and make thy name great; and thou shalt be a blessing: And I will bless them that bless thee, and curse him that curseth thee: and in thee shall all families of the earth be blessed.

We are first introduced to Abram in Genesis 11:27, as one of three brothers in the ninth generation from Shem, who was one of the three sons of Noah.

Abram's father, Terah, had moved the family to Haran, but that was not Abram's final destination.

As we see here in Genesis 12, God gave Abram specific instructions about leaving Ur to go to Canaan, the land He had promised to give them.

In Genesis 15:7, God reminded Abram, *"I am the Lord that brought thee out of Ur of the Chaldees, to give thee this land to inherit it."*

This is confirmed in Acts 7:2, when Stephen rehearsed Israel's history in front of the Jewish council:

> And he said, Men, brethren, and fathers, hearken; The God of glory appeared unto our father Abraham, when he was in Mesopotamia, before he dwelt in Charran [Haran].

People, Place, and Purpose

Abram's encounter with God is so important to the narrative I am sharing that I want to assure you that I am not being careless with the scriptural record.

As we consider the record of God's interactions with Abram (later known as Abraham), we see that there are three primary benefits that God announced to him: people, place, and purpose.

We are introduced to the *people* aspect in Genesis 12:1-3. God said that He would use Abram to make a great nation. What is particularly important is that by this time we have already learned that Abram's wife, Sarai, was childless (see Genesis 11:30).

Here is an incredible thing—a man whose wife was barren received a promise from God, whom he had never met and did not know heretofore, that he would become the progenitor of a great nation. There was no indication of when or how this would or could happen, yet Abram believed it!

The *place* aspect of God's promise was made in Genesis 15:7, which we have also already seen: Abram was to travel to a specific place, the land God was promising to give him. These first two promises went hand in hand. It would take a lot of people to occupy the land that God was giving them. It was certainly not something Abram could do on his own.

Now he had the promise of a people and a land where they could all live.

However, the remainder of Genesis 15 adds detail to this promise. Abram and God become involved in a covenant ceremony, which is described in Genesis 15:9-17. The burning lamp mentioned in this passage represents the presence of God, who passed between the pieces of the sacrifices in a solemn and binding agreement.

I want to particularly point out what God said next, in Genesis 15:18-21:

> In the same day the Lord made a covenant with Abram, saying, Unto thy seed have I given this land, from the river of Egypt unto the great river, the river Euphrates: The Kenites, and the Kenizzites, and the Kadmonites, and the Hittites, and the Perizzites, and the Rephaims, and the Amorites, and the Canaanites, and the Girgashites, and the Jebusites.

Not only did God give Abram the boundaries of the land his descendants were to *possess,* but He also told Abram that his descendants would *dispossess* the various Canaanites who were already living there. All these promises were made before Abram had even one descendant. God was already talking to him as though he were the father of the multitude God had already promised.

We also find the *purpose* aspect of God's covenant with Abram in Genesis 12. Genesis 12:2-3 says:

> And I will make of thee a great nation, and I will bless thee, and make thy name great; and thou shalt be a blessing: And I will bless them that bless thee, and curse him that curseth thee: and in thee shall all families of the earth be blessed.

This covenant promise is reiterated in Genesis 18:17-18:

> And the Lord said, Shall I hide from Abraham that thing which I do; seeing that Abraham shall surely become a great and mighty nation, and all the nations of the earth shall be blessed in him?

By this time, God had already changed Abram's name to Abraham, and his wife's name from Sarai to Sarah. If this were not enough, God spells out Abraham's purpose again in Genesis 22:18: *"And in thy seed shall all the nations of the earth be blessed; because thou hast obeyed my voice."*

When God makes a promise once, that is sufficient: He is God, and He cannot lie. When He rehearses that promise a second time, it emphasizes its importance. When He reiterates it a third time, it reminds us that it is a promise of eternal significance.

The following is a summary of the three aspects of God's covenant blessing to Abraham:

1. First, **people**: God said that Abraham would be the father of a great nation—a people too numerous to count. That nation is now known as the Jews.
2. Next, **place**: God said He would give Abraham's descendants a place to live and thrive—the land of Canaan. This is the Jewish homeland forever (see Genesis 13:15). This is a promise made by God, not by diplomats or politicians.
3. Finally, **purpose**: God said that the reason for His blessing upon Abraham and his descendants was so that they would be a blessing to the nations of the world. Without considering the many natural blessings Jewish people have given to the world, the singular blessing to which God is referring is that out of the Jewish nation would come the Messiah, the Lord Jesus Christ, the Savior of the world.

Let me point out something that cannot be emphasized enough—not one of these three benefits that God gave to Abraham (often referred to as the Abrahamic covenant) was ever repealed, retracted, recalled, voided, nullified, or otherwise altered in any way.

Those benefits are still just as valid now as when God spoke them into existence. Even though Abraham is no longer living, the promises that God made were not just to him, but to his descendants. Abraham's descendants (the Jews) are still very much alive, and that means the promises that God made to them live on.

Abraham was not a perfect man by any means. He made some grave errors of judgment in his lifetime, and the repercussions of at least one of those errors affect world events on a daily basis even now in the 21st century (Isaac and Ishmael, see Genesis 16).

However, Abraham believed God. That is what enabled him to move beyond his faults and find grace in God's sight. That is also why he is still rightly regarded as the Father of our Faith (see Romans 4:16).

God's Plan for the Nation of Israel

Let me move on to mention three additional aspects of God's purpose for the nation of Israel, as it was known from the time of the Exodus from Egypt. God intended Israel to be:

1. Custodians of the truth
2. Examples of the truth
3. Evangels of the truth

Of course, Israel had a spotty record of success in fulfilling these functions, but that does not negate the reality of God's intention for them as a nation among the nations of the world through their history.

Custodians of the truth: The custodian aspect is perhaps the easiest to identify. Israel was given the weighty responsibility of receiving God's law as they assembled at the foot of Mount Sinai shortly after their deliverance from Egyptian bondage. They accepted this responsibility as a body of people, having been charged by God and by Moses at the mountain. Exodus 24:7-8 says:

> And he took the book of the covenant, and read in the audience of the people: and they said, All that the Lord hath said will we do, and be obedient. And Moses took the blood, and sprinkled it on the people, and said, Behold the blood of the covenant, which the Lord hath made with you concerning all these words.

Examples of the truth: The law of God was more than just two tablets of stone, or the five books of Moses. God intended that His law be held in their hearts, heard in their speech, and lived out in their behavior. Deuteronomy 6:6-7 says:

> And these words, which I command thee this day, shall be in thine heart: And thou shalt teach them diligently unto thy children, and shalt talk of them when

> thou sittest in thine house, and when thou walkest by the way, and when thou liest down, and when thou risest up.

They were to keep it, cherish it, and never let it go.

The results of Israel's charge to be examples of truth varied as time went on. They were, after all, imperfect people (as all people are, with One notable exception!), and they were incapable of complying with all the requirements of the law. That is why God instituted a system of substitutionary sacrifices to cover their transgressions.

It was a rather elaborate system, overseen by the priests. Participation was uneven at best. Throughout Israel's history, times of apostasy would be interrupted by times of national repentance and revival. This cycle went on through the centuries, but seemed to gain less spiritual altitude with every cycle.

One reason for this may be that when truth that results in freedom is received, it generally hardens into a conviction in the hearts of those who receive it. They will not compromise, and they will not give up their hold on the truth.

They count it as precious, and they will not abandon it without a fight. In fact, they would rather die than relinquish the truth, since it was the truth that brought them the life they now enjoy.

The next generation often regards the truth as a persuasion rather than a conviction. They are often removed from the conditions that existed before the truth became known and produced freedom for their forebearers. As a result, they can be easily persuaded that something else is true.

The further removed they become from the privation that their forefathers endured, and the less aware they are of the sacrifices that were necessary to obtain the truth, the more likely it is that they will be open to persuasion.

By the third generation, what was once considered a conviction or a persuasion can become nothing more than an opinion. Everyone's opinion is given equal weight, regardless of its veracity or credibility. This creates an atmosphere where what was once regarded as the truth is counted as nothing more than a convenience. If an opinion becomes inconvenient for any reason, it can be easily discarded or exchanged for another opinion that is more popular or prevalent.

Evangels of the truth: Israel's behavior as evangels of truth is perhaps the most difficult to pinpoint of all.

The following is one indication of this purpose, from Deuteronomy 20:10-11:

> When thou comest nigh unto a city to fight against it, then proclaim peace unto it. And it shall be, if it make thee answer of peace, and open unto thee, then it

> shall be, that all the people that is found therein shall be tributaries unto thee, and they shall serve thee.

This instruction was for cities that lay beyond where the Canaanites lived. Israel had been instructed to destroy the Canaanites completely. Their failure to do so caused many problems for them in the future.

This created a situation that they would need to manage carefully, since Israel was supposed to be separate from other nations, and to maintain their distinctiveness at all costs. This principle was to keep them from being assimilated into other people groups, which would have made them indistinguishable from those around them, thus frustrating the plan of God for them as a people.

The Lineage of the Messiah

However, we must not overlook the reality that there were those from other nations who did decide to worship the true and living God. These people—called *proselytes*—became accepted as part of God's people.

That those from other lands and belief systems would worship the true God was only a prophetic foreshadowing of what would happen in the future. First, it would happen in the life and ministry of the Lord Jesus Christ. Next, it would happen in the ministry of His disciples in the book of Acts. Now, it is happening today as revival spreads around the earth. Finally, it will happen during the great ingathering of the end times.

There are a number of specific examples I could mention, but here is one notable case where a certain proselyte became part of the direct lineage of the Messiah. Ruth 4:13 says: *"So Boaz took Ruth, and she was his wife: and when he went in unto her, the Lord gave her conception, and she bare a son."*

The book of Ruth details the story of Ruth, a Moabite maiden, who married into the family of Naomi, an Israelite. When both Ruth's husband and Naomi's husband died, rather than return to her people, Ruth chose to accompany Naomi back to Bethlehem, Naomi's hometown.

There, Ruth married Boaz, a descendant of the tribe of Judah, and lived as a proselyte in the land of Israel. Their son, referred to in Ruth 4:13, was Obed, who became the grandfather of David, king of Israel. And we know that the lineage of King David led directly to the birth of the Messiah.

Throughout the historical sweep of the Old Testament, we see different pronouncements by God and His designated representatives that bring more and more clarity to the question of the Messiah's appearance.

As we have seen, God created a nation from Abraham's descendants. They began to be organized as a nation at Mount Sinai after their deliverance from Egypt. We see this from the arrangement of the tribes around the tabernacle in the wilderness, the institution of the sacrificial system, the organization of the priesthood, and the giving of the Law. God, in essence, was telling them, "Since you are going to be My people, this is how I expect you to live."

However, their identity as a distinct group of God-worshipers had begun much earlier. One of several defining moments came when Jacob and all his family moved to Egypt to avoid the famine that had affected so many lands at that time.

He and all his family uprooted themselves from their historic homeland and moved to a strange land, but they did not lose their identity, even in the midst of extremity.

Another significant milestone occurred before Jacob died. He delivered a prophetic proclamation to each of his sons. One of these proclamations identified the tribe from whom an eventual lawgiver would come. That honor belonged to the tribe of Judah. Here it is from Genesis 49:10: *"The sceptre shall not depart from Judah, nor a lawgiver from between his feet, until Shiloh come; and unto him shall the gathering of the people be."*

Much later, God narrowed the focus even further when He pointed out a particular family within the tribe of Judah who would produce the promised and eternal King. Second Samuel 7:13 says regarding Solomon: *"He shall build an house for my name, and I will stablish the throne of his kingdom for ever."*

We must not forget that the promise God made to Solomon was reiterating a promise previously made to King David.

Second Samuel 7:16 goes further, regarding David: *"And thine house and thy kingdom shall be established for ever before thee: thy throne shall be established for ever."*

There is an apparent contradiction to this promise found in the book of Jeremiah, which I will discuss in the following chapter. Suffice it to say that God keeps His promises, regardless of how unlikely they may seem, or how undeserving those who receive them may appear to be.

Here is one more detail that further proscribes the boundaries of the promised Redeemer's advent—God revealed the place where He would be born. Micah 5:2 says:

> But thou, Bethlehem Ephratah, though thou be little among the thousands of Judah, yet out of thee shall he come forth unto me that is to be ruler in Israel; whose goings forth have been from of old, from everlasting.

This was well known to the scholars of the law at the time of Jesus' birth. They referenced this passage when King Herod asked where the King of the Jews would be born (see Matthew 2:1-6).

You may be wondering what all this has to do with replacement theology, since it may seem as though I have gone far afield from that discussion. The revelation God provided about *through whom* and *where* the promised Messiah would be born gave our adversary the information he thought he needed to snuff out Jesus' life before it began.

Herod made this decree, found in Matthew 2:16-18:

> Then Herod, when he saw that he was mocked of the wise men, was exceeding wroth, and sent forth, and slew all the children that were in Bethlehem, and in all the coasts thereof, from two years old and under, according to the time which he had diligently inquired of the wise men. Then was fulfilled that which was spoken by Jeremiah the prophet, saying, In Rama was there a voice heard, lamentation, and weeping, and great mourning, Rachel weeping for her children, and would not be comforted, because they are not.

Of course, we realize from our vantage point far removed from these developments that Jesus and His family were long gone from Bethlehem by the time this ungodly decree was carried out.

Remember, the end result of replacement theology is antisemitism. Even though replacement theology may be a relative newcomer to the field of antisemitism, the fruit of its doctrine is not a new development. It has existed for thousands of years.

Although humans are involved in its proliferation, antisemitism in all its forms is not, and has never been, of human origin. It is a plan devised by the devil and his associates. All those who participate in it, whether or not they realize it, are partaking of a diabolical plot, conceived in darkness, to circumvent the plan of God for human history.

LIE #3

THE LIE OF THE BROKEN RELATIONSHIP

The covenant God made with Abraham and his descendants has never been revoked or repealed. This is particularly incredible when considering the unfaithfulness of the ancient nation of Israel in maintaining their end of the covenant agreement, especially when their unfaithfulness landed them time after time in bondage.

Their bondage in Egypt, though, was as a result of other factors. One of these factors was specifically to fulfill the prophecy found in Genesis 15:13. This prophecy said that Abraham and his descendants would be strangers in a foreign land and would be enslaved and oppressed for 400 years.

Joseph's position in Egypt served to protect them during a time of famine; but as the people multiplied and a new

Pharaoh came into power, it was time to shake off the Egyptian bondage and enter their Promised Land.

We see in the book of Exodus that God's purpose was to bring Israel out of their enslavement in a foreign land and into the land that He had promised to Abraham many years before.

The plagues that came upon Egypt were not just to convince Pharaoh to let Israel go. They were also to convince Israel that they could trust God to lead them into an unknown future.

God's problem was twofold: *He had to get Israel out of Egypt, and He also had to get Egypt out of Israel*. What I mean by that is that the habits, tendencies, and patterns that Israel had adopted for generations of captivity had to be replaced with obedience to a God they could not see and with whom they were not familiar. They had no sooner left their enemies drowned in the Red Sea that the murmuring began.

Moses Intercedes for His People

Moses had been tasked with the responsibility to lead this bunch (millions of them) through a hostile desert to a land filled with Canaanites. They made it to Mount Sinai, not without their share of difficulties at the outset. It was there that they provoked God to the point of judgment with the golden calf incident (see Exodus 32–34).

Think of the magnitude of this audacious and impertinent rebellion. God had clearly spoken to them in Exodus 20:3-6:

> Thou shalt have no other gods before me. Thou shalt not make unto thee any graven image, or any likeness of any thing that is in heaven above, or that is in the earth beneath, or that is in the water under the earth. Thou shalt not bow down thyself to them, nor serve them: for I, the Lord thy God am a jealous God, visiting the iniquity of the fathers upon the children unto the third and fourth generation of them that hate me; and shewing mercy unto thousands of them that love me, and keep my commandments.

There was no room for debate or dissension here. Yet, not much more than a month later, Israel had flagrantly disregarded the first two commandments God had given them. They had what amounted to a wild and probably drunken party, worshiping a graven image that was the very thing God had expressly forbidden them to do!

God essentially said He would remove them all and start over with Moses. However, instead of accepting that, Moses interceded for the entire nation, and God heard and answered him.

There were two other occasions when Moses stood between Israel and swift and certain judgment. One was after

Israel refused to go into the Promised Land after the spies came back from their mission into Canaan (see Numbers 14). The other was after the rebellion of Korah, Dathan, and Abiram (see Numbers 16).

With these incidents in mind, it is a wonder that they made it to the Promised Land at all. In fact, all but two of an entire generation died during the wilderness wanderings due to disobedience.

You Can't Curse What God Has Blessed

There is one more incident during this period that I need to mention. Balak, king of the Moabites, hired Balaam the seer to curse Israel as they passed near Balak's dominion during their journey.

Three times Balak urged Balaam to curse Israel, and three times Balaam was unable to do so.

Finally, he told the Moabite king, in essence, "I can't curse what God has blessed" (see Numbers 24:9).

We see a footnote to this episode in Numbers 31:16, when Moses reprimanded the leaders of Israel for saving some Midianites from destruction (you can look back to Numbers 25 for an explanation of this trespass and its consequences):

> Behold, these caused the children of Israel, through the counsel of Balaam, to commit trespass against the

> Lord in the matter of Peor, and there was a plague among the congregation of the Lord.

Balaam could not curse Israel, but he did advise the king of Moab about how Israel could be tempted to bring a curse on themselves because of disobedience. The perpetrators died, but the nation survived and continued to move forward to occupy their inheritance, which was the land of Canaan. Israel could not be overcome from without, but it could be thwarted from within.

I cannot elaborate on all the apostasies that occurred in the book of Judges, except to say that they all followed the same pattern, which was fourfold:

1. Bondage
2. Repentance
3. Deliverance
4. Freedom

God's mercy was on full display throughout this period in Israel's history. After all that, and partly as a result of it, Israel demanded an earthly king. God didn't want them to have a king, but eventually He gave them what they demanded.

The result was a terrible bargain. Saul acted as a deliverer, but before his reign was over, he was far more obsessed with killing David than he was with opposing his enemies the Philistines.

The kingdom of Israel was finally established under David, and later under Solomon. It was during Solomon's reign that Israel came to its zenith of power and prosperity.

Disobedience Leads to Division and Disorder

However, the seeds of destruction were already sown because of Solomon's proclivity for three things God said that the kings of Israel must not multiply: wives, horses, and gold. Deuteronomy 17:16-17 says:

> But he shall not multiply horses to himself, nor cause the people to return to Egypt, to the end that he should multiply horses: forasmuch as the Lord hath said unto you, Ye shall henceforth return no more that way. Neither shall he multiply wives to himself, that his heart turn not away: neither shall he greatly multiply to himself silver and gold.

Solomon did all three, and his kingdom was divided in the days of his son Rehoboam. From that time onward, the northern kingdom was known as Israel and the southern kingdom was known as Judah.

The trajectories of the two kingdoms can be summarized by steady decline. In the southern kingdom, some reformers, such as Jehoshaphat and Josiah, slowed the descent. Finally, the northern kingdom was carried away into captivity by the Assyrians. Then, 136 years later, Judah went into captivity to Babylon.

Conditions became so bad, and the apostasy was so widespread, and the rebellion was so complete that God made this startling announcement in Jeremiah 22:29-30:

> O earth, earth, earth, hear the word of the Lord. Thus saith the Lord, Write ye this man ***childless***, a man that shall not prosper in his days: for no man of his seed shall prosper, sitting upon the throne of David, and ruling any more in Judah.

The man who would be childless and have no heir to sit on the throne of his ancestor David was Coniah (also known as Jechoniah or Jehoiachin), the son of Jehoiakim, the son of Josiah, who was the last good king of Judah.

You may remember that God said that David's throne would be established perpetually. How is it, then, that God would disrupt this order and declare that the rulers of Judah would have no more heirs to sit on the throne?

That is a legitimate question that has a solidly scriptural answer, although one that is beyond the scope of this book. Without dwelling on the details, know that Jesus, rightfully called the son of David, had and has a perfectly legitimate and legal claim to the throne of David, without complication or compromise.

An individual's wickedness, or a city's wickedness, or a nation's wickedness ultimately cannot and will not thwart the plan of God. Jeremiah 31:35-37 says:

> Thus saith the Lord, which giveth the sun for a light by day, and the ordinances of the moon and of the stars for a light by night, which divideth the sea when the waves thereof roar; The Lord of hosts is his name: If those ordinances depart from before me, saith the Lord, then the seed of Israel also shall cease from being a nation before me for ever. Thus saith the Lord; If heaven above can be measured, and the foundations of the earth searched out beneath, I will also cast off all the seed of Israel for all that they have done, saith the Lord.

Some people would be so bold as to ask why the God who is supposed to represent love and tolerance would judge nations so severely. We risk two errors when we travel that road.

The first is that we do not have the right to question why God does what He does any more than the clay has the right to question the potter's purpose (see Jeremiah 18:3-6 and Romans 9:20).

The second is that if God has no right to execute righteous judgment, then justice itself has no guarantor and we are left in a world where wrong is never ultimately made right. The world then becomes a place where accountability is an illusion and wrongs go permanently unanswered.

It may not be necessary to remind you that every timepiece or calendar you have ever consulted depends upon a reliable and stable universe. Every bridge you travel across—whether on your way home through a tree-lined street or when traveling on a multilane highway—depends on certain immutable engineering principles. You don't even think about them as you travel, but you depend on them, nonetheless. What I am saying is that God created an ordered universe, not a random one.

Even further, if we say the universe is out of order, we are saying that there is no hope for justice in the world at any time or on any level. This is an indefensible and dangerous position that will ultimately lead to nihilism, which is the belief that nothing matters.

Nihilism also leads people to barbaric behavior. If there are no consequences to wrongdoing—indeed, if the very concepts of right and wrong are only arbitrary and artificial—then let us do whatever we want, whenever we want, however we want, and to whomever we want.

No society can survive for very long under those conditions or that belief system. Every vestige of civic order would break down and disappear overnight, and the only thing that would be certain is chaos.

Even a casual reading of the Bible reveals that Israel's behavior was so bad that God had to distance Himself from them by judgment. Even the heathen recognized that. The following is the testimony of a Babylonian official to the prophet Jeremiah after the fall of Jerusalem, from Jeremiah 40:2-3:

> And the captain of the guard took Jeremiah, and said unto him, The Lord thy God hath pronounced this evil upon this place. Now the Lord hath brought it, and done according as he hath said: because ye have sinned against the Lord, and have not obeyed his voice, therefore this thing is come upon you.

He Is Faithful

The entire book of Hosea, another one of the prophets of Israel, became a metaphor about the nation of Israel and the God she had forsaken. The book reveals the depth of depravity to which Israel, the backslider, had sunk.

Judgment would surely come upon such backslidings as these, and yet God summarizes His attitude toward them in Hosea 14:4-6:

> I will heal their backsliding, I will love them freely: for mine anger is turned away from him. I will be as the dew unto Israel: he shall grow as the lily, and cast

> forth his roots as Lebanon. His branches shall spread, and his beauty shall be as the olive tree, and his smell as Lebanon.

How could a just God continue to love and bless such a backsliding people? Hear this, from Ezekiel 36:22-24:

> Therefore say unto the house of Israel, thus saith the Lord God; I do not this for your sakes, O house of Israel, but for mine holy name's sake, which ye have profaned among the heathen, whither ye went. And I will sanctify my great name, which was profaned among the heathen, which ye have profaned in the midst of them; and the heathen shall know that I am the Lord, saith the Lord God, when I shall be sanctified in you before their eyes. For I will take you from among the heathen, and gather you out of all countries, and will bring you into your own land.

God did not extend His mercy to Israel because of their faithfulness—they had none. *He did it because He is faithful.* Second Timothy 2:12-13 echoes this thought:

> If we suffer, we shall also reign with him: if we deny him, he also will deny us: If we believe not, yet he abideth faithful: he cannot deny himself.

Here is one more witness, from Jeremiah 29:11:

> For I know the thoughts that I think toward you, saith the Lord, thoughts of peace, and not of evil, to give you an expected end.

God was speaking to the discouraged exiles in Babylon. He told them that after 70 years had transpired, He would arrange for them to return to the home He had given them. It must have seemed not only unlikely, but impossible. Yet, it happened just as God said it would.

Despite Israel violating every commandment, breaking every law, and disrespecting every righteous principle that God gave them, He still claimed them as His own. The proof of that is that He brought them back to the land from which they had been taken by their captors. It was improbable, it was a miracle. Yet, history unfolds as the prophets foretold.

Shifting the Blame

Now it is time to turn the focus away from Israel and onto ourselves.

Could it be that one of the motivations for replacement theology is that people want to blame Israel for its bad behavior while excusing their own bad behavior?

Are they whistling in the dark, hoping to avoid God's righteous judgment, while engaging in the same things they condemn in others? Has there been a beam in their eye while they are searching out the speck in the eyes of those around them or around the globe from them?

Let me go a step further and for a moment leave aside the proponents of replacement theology. What about the Christian churches? There are tens of thousands of denominations worldwide, with hundreds of different kinds of churches right here in America.

Jesus prayed that we would be unified as one, but it seems as though we try to do everything in our power to remain split and splintered. Division is a strategy of the devil, and weakens anything that is divided. Unity is a principle of the Kingdom of God, and leads to strength.

Why, then, do we find it impossible to agree about anything, even the most fundamental tenets of faith or practice? Isn't that one reason that the Church is weak when it should be strong? How can the Church that is fractured rather than united show the world who God really is?

Jesus said in Matthew 5:13:

> Ye are the salt of the earth: but if the salt have lost his savour, wherewith shall it be salted? it is thenceforth good for nothing, but to be cast out, and to be trodden under foot of men.

The primary use of salt is to either preserve or flavor food. Salt can lose its saltiness, so to speak, through exposure to the elements. Believers are supposed to be the salt of the earth.

What happens when we lose our distinctiveness, and become just like the world out of which God has called us? According to Jesus, we are good for nothing, and are likely to be cast out and trodden under foot.

Is that one reason that so many believers and so many churches are despised instead of respected? Have we lost our collective saltiness? Have we become just like everyone else? If we have, it should come as no surprise that we are ridiculed and rejected—not because we are different from the world, but because we are just like the world to which we are supposed to provide a desirable contrast.

What will it take to bring us to our collective senses, and help us come to a place of repentance and faith so that instead of trembling at the onslaught of hell, the gates of hell will not prevail against us?

Will our behavior get so bad that God will have to judge us, so that His name is vindicated? Do we think that will not happen to us? What makes us think so? Has God changed? Is our present-day sin any less reprehensible than the idolatry of ancient Israel?

Even Moses, to whom God spoke as a man speaks to a friend, was not exempt from judgment. In Numbers 20:2-13,

Moses was commanded to speak to the rock, but he struck it instead, and rebuked the congregation. God said that Moses would not be allowed to go into the Promised Land because he did not obey in this instance.

God was not involved in the striking and the rebuking, so He separated Himself from Moses. Do we think God won't do the same to us if we refuse to obey His instructions?

We should thank God that the steadfast love of the Lord never ceases, and that His mercies are new every morning (see Lamentations 3:22-23). And if we thank God that His commitment to us has not changed due to our iniquity, how can we say that God's commitment to Israel has changed due to her iniquity, either past or present? When it comes right down to it, God's faithfulness depends on Him, not on us.

Some who currently disparage everything related to Israel and the Jews will undoubtedly say, "I'm just asking questions." If all they do is ask the wrong questions, all they will get is wrong answers. The question is not *what about them,* the question is *what about you!* Besides that, the questioners certainly seem and sound like they have already come to very certain conclusions (rather than just asking questions to gather information *before* coming to any conclusion).

Where does that leave us? Did Israel forfeit its covenant through disobedience? God forbid! We had better hope that

Israel succeeds and flourishes. Because if God made an everlasting covenant with Israel and they fail, what hope do we have that His everlasting covenant with us will withstand the perils of perilous times? Stay with me; I will discuss this principle further in the pages that follow.

LIE #4

THE LIE OF THE ABSENT GOD

By now, he thought he had seen and experienced everything he could possibly see and experience. Many episodes in his life could be called strange and even bizarre. They were certainly far beyond what any normal person would consider ordinary or usual. But this one surpassed them all.

He was not certain whether this was a dream, a vision, or whether it was really happening to him. He didn't recognize where he was. The place seemed vaguely familiar, but he could not imagine where, or even if, he had seen it before.

One moment he was standing in the courtyard of his home; the next, he was in this vast valley. It was broad and multi-faceted—not narrow and constricted as most river valleys were. It was irregular in shape, and so large he could not see the ends of it.

The most remarkable feature about it was not its size or its scope—it was what was in it. The valley he was looking at was full of human bones.

Replacement theology maintains that God is essentially finished with Israel and that they are unnecessary and irrelevant. Nothing could be further from the truth. To those who think that Israel will ultimately be relegated to the dustbin of history, I offer this passage, which proves that God can bring not just individuals, but a nation back from the dead.

As you read, take note how many times the word *live* is used. Ezekiel 37:1-14 declares:

> The hand of the Lord was upon me, and carried me out in the spirit of the Lord, and set me down in the midst of the valley which was full of bones, and caused me to pass by them round about: and, behold, there were very many in the open valley; and, lo, they were very dry. And he said unto me, Son of man, can these bones ***live***?
>
> And I answered, O Lord God, thou knowest. Again he said unto me, Prophesy upon these bones, and say

unto them, O ye dry bones, hear the word of the Lord. Thus saith the Lord God unto these bones; Behold, I will cause breath to enter into you, and ye shall ***live***:

And I will lay sinews upon you, and will bring up flesh upon you, and cover you with skin, and put breath in you, and ye shall ***live***; and ye shall know that I am the Lord. So I prophesied as I was commanded: and as I prophesied, there was a noise, and behold a shaking, and the bones came together, bone to his bone.

And when I beheld, lo, the sinews and the flesh came up upon them, and the skin covered them above: but there was no breath in them. Then said he unto me, Prophesy unto the wind, prophesy, son of man, and say to the wind, Thus saith the Lord God; Come from the four winds, O breath, and breathe upon these slain, that they may ***live***.

So I prophesied as he commanded me, and the breath came into them, and they ***lived***, and stood up upon their feet, an exceeding great army. Then he said unto me, Son of man, these bones are the whole house of Israel: behold, they say, Our bones are dried, and our hope is lost: we are cut off for our parts. Therefore prophesy and say unto them, Thus saith the Lord God; Behold, O my people, I will open your graves,

> and cause you to come up out of your graves, and bring you into the land of Israel.
>
> And ye shall know that I am the Lord, when I have opened your graves, O my people, and brought you up out of your graves, and shall put my spirit in you, and ye shall ***live***, and I shall place you in your own land: then shall ye know that I the Lord have spoken it, and performed it, saith the Lord.

God has miraculously preserved His people throughout their history. Israel's story is a series of supernatural occurrences that has kept them from complete and utter annihilation, over and over again.

Even when the most powerful empires in the world were determined to destroy them utterly, they were never able to succeed. This cannot be the result of coincidence or random chance. It was and is the hand of God, the same hand of God that carried the prophet Ezekiel into the Valley of Dry Bones and showed him Israel's future. Examples of this abound. I will cite just a few.

Joseph: Joseph's older brothers were moved with envy against him. He was their father Jacob's favorite, and their anger toward Joseph finally manifested in their determination to kill him. They created the opportunity, and almost carried it out. At the last moment, the chance to profit from Joseph's life instead arose and stayed their hand: they sold him into slavery.

In the process of time, and unknown to his family, Joseph became the prime minister of Egypt. This was providential since it resulted in Jacob and his entire family being saved from starvation during a seven-year famine.

The Exodus: The Exodus from Egypt is well-known, and it has been depicted endlessly in stories, books, and films. It was the largest and most complete deliverance of one nation from another in human history. When you consider the series of events that transpired—including the Red Sea parting and dry land appearing, to the drowning of an entire army in a single moment—you can't help but see the supernatural intervention that took place.

The Promised Land: The conquest of Canaan is another example of the hand of God on Israel. From the fall of Jericho's impenetrable walls to the various campaigns waged by Joshua against the Canaanites, God dispossessed Israel's enemies and gave them a home in Canaan, the land He had promised to give them.

The return from exile: The return of the Jews to their homeland after the Babylonian exile is another example of God's divine favor toward Israel. Not only did they return to their homeland, but they also rebuilt the temple and the city of Jerusalem.

The Maccabean revolt: Israel has always been situated at the crossroads of three continents. Europe, Asia, and Africa have all sent armies into the region for conquest or defense. Israel was often at the mercy of whatever army was in the area.

After the death of Alexander the Great, when the Syrian occupation resulted in Antiochus Epiphanes slaughtering a sow on the altar of the temple, the Jews revolted. Under the leadership of the Maccabees, and against overwhelming odds, they were successful in overthrowing Syrian rule and establishing an independent nation, known as the Hasmonean Dynasty.

The uprising against the Syrians began in 167 BC and resulted in full political autonomy in 142 BC. That arrangement lasted until 63 BC, when the Romans made Israel a client state. I might add that this development was only made possible by civil war between two Hasmonean leaders (who were brothers) who fought each other for the right to rule.

The Resurrection: The Jews chafed under the restrictions of Roman administration. Messianic fervor often coalesced behind a charismatic leader who would gather and lead a band of idealistic followers that lasted until his untimely and often violent demise.

This happened during the life of a man from Nazareth named Jesus. As you know, He was betrayed, crucified, and buried in a borrowed tomb, only to rise from the dead. These developments were the turning point of history, but to the Romans, they constituted nothing more than another incident in the restive backwater province of Judea.

Jerusalem captured, but reconfigured: Far worse troubles were on the horizon. A Jewish revolt that began in AD 66 resulted in the destruction of the temple in AD 70 and the building of a pagan temple in its place. Later, in AD 132, Simon Bar Kochba led another revolt that was ultimately crushed by Rome.

In the aftermath, Jews were barred from entering Jerusalem on pain of death. The city of Jerusalem was renamed Aelia Capitolina, and it was reimagined and resettled as a Roman city instead of a Jewish one. This was just one of the efforts to erase the Jews from their homeland.

Although Jerusalem was now occupied by a Roman population, the city itself was still there, waiting for the eventual return of the Jews.

In a continued effort to eradicate the Jews, multiplied thousands of Jews were killed, or sold into slavery, accelerating their dispersion into the nations of the world, thus fulfilling prophecy.

Hitler's Holocaust: The attitude toward Jews in many parts of the world resulted in suspicion, alienation, and often violence. I have summarized much of this in Chapter 1. The result of this was Hitler's "Final Solution," where he and others under his leadership decided they would rid the world of the Jews once and for all. They were ultimately unsuccessful, but it was not for lack of effort.

Israel declared a nation: As the horrifying details of the Holocaust became known and undeniable after the end of World War II, momentum increased among the nations to allow the Jews to find a homeland. The obvious choice was their ancestral home. Problematically, it was already occupied by others.

The British government had received a mandate from the now moribund League of Nations to administrate the region of Palestine. That mandate ended May 14, 1948.

That same day, Israel declared itself a sovereign nation, and the American president, Harry Truman, recognized their government. The next day, five nations surrounding Israel declared war against her, intending to wipe the new nation from the earth.

How Israel fought five other nations to a standstill in nine months is a story in itself—actually many stories, most or all of which have remarkably spectacular elements. Israel prevailed and signed armistices with all the belligerent nations in 1949.

The Suez Canal: I must mention Israel's military involvement in the Suez Canal crisis of 1956 before going further, because it directly impacted what happened in Israel nine years later. In July 1956, the Egyptian president, Gamal Abdel Nasser, nationalized the Suez Canal, effectively ending Britain and France's control of that waterway, and bringing it solely under Egyptian governance.

This created an impossible situation since most of Europe's oil passed through the canal on tankers. Britain, France, and Israel developed a plan whereby Israel would invade the Sinai Peninsula, and Britain and France would intervene, supposedly to keep Israel and Egypt from entering into a wider conflict.

In the process, Britain and France planned to regain control of the Suez Canal, and hoped to depose Nasser in the process. Israel did what they said they would do, and occupied much of Sinai and Gaza, but US and Soviet pressure kept Britain and France from following through with their plans.

Because of that, Israel withdrew in March 1957, with the conditions that Egypt would not interfere with Israeli shipping through the Straits of Tiran (the access point to the Red Sea), and that a UN peacekeeping force would be stationed between Egypt and Israel.

The Six-Day War: These conditions prevailed until Egypt blockaded Straits of Tiran to ships bound for Israel in May

1967. Israeli oil supplies from Iran used this route, and this action by Egypt threatened Israel's oil supply. This breach of trust by Egypt was considered by Israel to be an act of war.

In addition, Egypt ordered the UN peacekeeping force to leave and began moving military vehicles and troops to the Sinai Peninsula. At the same time, Jordan and Syria began military mobilization east and north of Israel.

Facing a naval blockade and what seemed like aggression on three fronts, Israel launched a preemptive air strike against Egypt's air forces and destroyed most of them on the first day of the conflict that became known as the Six-Day War. During this action, Israel took four regions: the Sinai Peninsula; Gaza; the West Bank, including the eastern portion of the city of Jerusalem; and the Golan Heights. This in itself was no small miracle, considering that enemy troops were stationed *above* them on the Golan Heights, and they had to fight their way *up* to gain victory.

The Yom Kippur War: Conditions remained tense until war broke out again when Egypt and Syria both attempted to regain control of territory that had been occupied by Israel since 1967. Their military actions began on October 6, 1973, which was Yom Kippur, the Day of Atonement, the most holy and solemn day in Israel, and a national holiday.

Israel was taken by surprise, and most of its military personnel were observing the holiday. They found themselves fighting desperately on two fronts, both north and south. The war lasted for 19 days until a UN-sponsored ceasefire went into effect.

This conflict and its aftermath led to the signing of the Camp David Accords between Egypt and Israel in 1978, and the Egypt-Israel peace treaty of 1979. In return for their withdrawal from the Sinai Peninsula, Israel was recognized as a legitimate state by Egypt—the first Arab nation to do so.

Recent Developments: There have been other convulsions and military actions by Israel since then, mostly against Hezbollah in the north and Hamas in the south. Palestinian unrest reached its zenith on October 7, 2023, when more than 5,000 Hamas fighters made an incursion into southern Israel and killed more than 1,200 Israelis and took 250 people hostage. It was the single deadliest day in Jewish history since the Holocaust. Israel's response to this attack was to move into Gaza with the purpose of disarming and disbanding Hamas.

I have taken time to rehearse some historical events in Israel's history for two purposes. The *first reason* is to point out that if God had been finished with Israel, He could have at multiple points throughout their history very easily allowed them to be destroyed. As current events attest, Israel is very much alive and a permanent part of the modern world.

If the proponents of replacement theology are correct, why is Israel still a functioning state on earth? No other people group on earth has had such a long and agonizing history as the Jews—dispersed, hated, scorned, ridiculed, falsely accused, disregarded, victimized, slaughtered—and yet they are still standing. Natural explanations, regardless of how fanciful or far-fetched they may seem, cannot explain the obvious fact that Israel still survives, and their survival is a miracle.

The answer is, or at least should be, obvious. God is involved in the preservation and protection of His people. He made a covenant with Abraham and Abraham's descendants, and that covenant is still in force today.

This is the *second reason* I recounted Israel's history. I have made this point before, but it deserves repeating. Every believer should thank God that He has been faithful to His covenant to Israel since that has a direct effect on their lives.

Think of it this way: if God had abandoned His commitment to Israel, how could any believer in Christ as Savior be confident that God would stand by them during times of difficulty and danger? In contrast, look at the times God rescued Israel from what looked like total eradication. He always enabled them to rebound and reassemble. That means that regardless of what you are facing or fighting right now, God is committed to giving His endless supply of help to you. In the midst of your darkest midnight, you can confidently call upon Him, and He will hear and answer.

A Beautiful Bride

Two incidents come to my mind that prove this beyond question. One is from ancient history, and one took place less than 80 years ago.

Long ago, a Persian king threw a party that lasted six months. During the last week of this revelry, the king commanded the queen to come to the party so he could show her off to his inebriated guests. The queen refused. The king was enraged, and on the counsel of his advisors, immediately deposed her.

The problem of a wife disobeying her husband's order was resolved, but another problem arose. Who would be the queen now that the former queen had been removed from her position?

Once again, the king sought counsel from his advisors. They recommended that the king hold a nationwide beauty pageant, and that the damsel who pleased him the most of all of them could be his new queen. Of course, the king thought that was a splendid idea.

The pageant winner turned out to be a young woman who surpassed all the others in grace and beauty. Unknown to the king and all his advisors, she was one of the captives of Judah, who had been assimilated into the Persian empire after the fall of Babylon. She became queen, with all the privileges and perquisites that went with being the wife of the most powerful man in the world.

In the process of time, one of the king's advisors, who took offense that a Jew outside the palace gate would not bow to him, hatched a plot to kill all the Jews in the empire. He received approval for his plan from the king while they were drinking together. The day was set, and the order was sent all over the empire.

The Jew outside the palace gate happened to be the guardian of the young woman who had recently become queen. He told the queen, whose given name was Hadassah, about the plot. She appealed to the king to stop the slaughter, and finally revealed that she was one of the people the murder plot had targeted.

The king wanted to know who was responsible for planning to murder his queen. She identified the man, and he was executed on the very gallows he had built on which he planned to hang the Jew who failed to bow to him earlier. Another decree was issued that allowed the Jews to defend themselves from all who would harm them. Thus, the nation was preserved from certain annihilation. You can read all the details in the book of Esther.

Arms and Ammunition

As I mentioned, Israel was also facing annihilation from five enemies immediately after they announced their statehood in 1948. They had precious little military equipment, and they were facing five armies that were far better supplied. What was even worse, there was an embargo in place that prevented any nation from sending arms to the Mideast. This was far more devastating to Israel than it was to the surrounding Arab nations, since those nations were already equipped.

Two ridiculously improbable series of events changed the equation for Israel.

First, a clandestine group in America arranged to purchase military surplus aircraft and fly them to Israel without the US government's knowledge. They used various extralegal means to achieve their objectives, and employed American pilots to ferry the aircraft to their destinations. These aircraft, at first mainly transport planes, became indispensable to Israel obtaining war supplies from the most unlikely of sources, as we shall see.

Even more incredibly, the only nation on earth that agreed to sell arms and ammunition to Israel was Czechoslovakia. That nation had recently undergone a coup that toppled their democratic government and installed a communist regime that soon fell under the umbrella of the Soviet Union.

Czechoslovakia was uniquely positioned for the task of providing war supplies to Israel. It had been the site of manufacturing facilities for the German war machine during World War II, and many of those arms were still in Czech warehouses.

The Czechs also had aircraft, based on the German designed ME-109 fighter. It was cobbled together with a different engine and other necessary design changes, which made it difficult and dangerous to fly. However, something was better than nothing, and those planes provided the only fighter aircraft that Israel could obtain in the early stages of their War of Independence.

How is it that the Soviets, of all people, allowed one of their satellite states to arm Israel? As incredible as it seems, the Soviet Union thought that if they allowed Czechoslovakia to supply Israel, it would tip the scales to cause Israel to align itself with the Soviet sphere of influence.

The Soviets were interested in weakening Britain's influence in the Middle East. They also wanted to provide a counter to some of the Arab monarchies' affinity for Britain. These calculations created an arrangement that was as unique as it was strange—the Soviet Union, through their client state, Czechoslovakia, was the only nation in the world who sold arms to the infant state of Israel! Without those desperately needed supplies, it is unlikely that Israel would have been able to resist the onslaught that they successfully repelled through 1948 and into 1949.

The existence of Israel today is a sign and a wonder, not a historical coincidence. God moved on both individuals and nations to preserve Israel at different points throughout their history. He will not forget His covenant promises. He will also remember His covenant when you are in distress and danger. Who knows what kinds of circumstances God is aligning in your favor during the darkest moments of your life?

It may look bad, but it will be infinitely worse if God does not intervene on your behalf. He is faithful, and we should remember to thank Him for His faithfulness every time we have an opportunity.

LIE #5

THE LIE OF THE MISSING PROPHECIES

Does Israel have any place in end-time prophecy? The answer seems obvious but not to many theologians and influencers today. Let's examine replacement theology in the light of Bible prophecy. As I plan to show, embracing replacement theology would require rewriting, or at least reimagining, many Scripture passages referring to end-time events, as well as most of the book of Revelation. We also look into the mystery of Daniel's 70th week and what it means for us today.

When seeking an understanding of apocalyptic literature, including passages in the Bible that deal with end-time events, we must keep consistent hermeneutical principles in mind. (*Hermeneutics* is a fancy term that theologians use that deals with how Bible texts are interpreted.)

Double Reference, Now and in the Future

One of these principles involves double reference. This is when one Bible passage refers to more than one event—the first is immediate, and the second is distant. Sometimes the distant event to which the Bible passage refers is hundreds or even thousands of years in the future. Of course, there is no way anyone can know what is going to happen that far ahead of time without the influence of the Holy Spirit giving them insight into future events.

One such example is Isaiah 7:10-16:

> Moreover the Lord spake again unto Ahaz, saying, Ask thee a sign of the Lord thy God; ask it either in the depth, or in the height above. But Ahaz said, I will not ask, neither will I tempt the Lord. And he said, Hear ye now, O house of David; Is it a small thing for you to weary men, but will ye weary my God also?
>
> Therefore the Lord himself shall give you a sign; Behold, a virgin shall conceive, and bear a son, and shall call his name Immanuel. Butter and honey shall he eat, that he may know to refuse the evil, and choose the good. For before the child shall know to refuse the evil, and choose the good, the land that thou abhorrest shall be forsaken of both her kings.

The context of this passage is the prophet Isaiah speaking words of encouragement to King Ahaz of Judah. The Word from the Lord said that Ahaz did not need to be concerned with the apparent threats from Syria and Ephraim (the northern kingdom of Israel), since both of their leaders would soon be gone. The immediate fulfillment of this prophecy occurred when both those kings were overthrown within a few years, before a child would know how to choose between good and evil.

The distant fulfillment of this prophetic word came many centuries later, when Jesus was born of a virgin in Bethlehem. Matthew 1:20-23 attests to this specifically:

> But while he thought on these things, behold, the angel of the Lord appeared unto him in a dream, saying, Joseph, thou son of David, fear not to take unto thee Mary thy wife: for that which is conceived in her is of the Holy Ghost. And she shall bring forth a son, and thou shalt call his name Jesus: for he shall save his people from their sins.
>
> Now all this was done, that it might be fulfilled which was spoken of the Lord by the prophet, saying, Behold, a virgin shall be with child, and shall bring forth a son, and they shall call his name Emmanuel, which being interpreted is, God with us.

Zion: Thou Art My People

Regarding Israel and the end times, consider this passage, which Jesus quoted from the prophet Isaiah in Luke 4:18-19:

> The Spirit of the Lord is upon me, because he hath anointed me to preach the gospel to the poor; he hath sent me to heal the brokenhearted, to preach deliverance to the captives, and recovering of sight to the blind, to set at liberty them that are bruised, to preach the acceptable year of the Lord.

At this point, Jesus stopped reading and closed the scroll. The reason for this was the remainder of the passage in Isaiah did not deal with His first advent, but with His return to the earth, 2,000 years and still counting later.

Here is the remainder of the passage, starting with the phrase from Isaiah 61:2 that picks up after Jesus finished reading, and ends with verse 6:

> ...and the day of vengeance of our God; to comfort all that mourn; To appoint unto them that mourn in Zion, to give unto them beauty for ashes, the oil of joy for mourning, the garment of praise for the spirit of heaviness; that they might be called trees of righteousness, the planting of the Lord, that he might be glorified.

> And they shall build the old wastes, they shall raise up the former desolations, and they shall repair the waste cities, the desolations of many generations. And strangers shall stand and feed your flocks, and the sons of the alien shall be your plowmen and your vinedressers.
>
> But ye shall be named the Priests of the Lord: men shall call you the Ministers of our God: ye shall eat the riches of the Gentiles, and in their glory shall ye boast yourselves (Isaiah 61:2-6).

Zion, as the term is used here, does not mean a hill and fortification that David captured in the Jebusite stronghold of ancient Jebus, later known as Jerusalem. Zion means the nation of Israel. For additional proof, notice Isaiah 51:16: *"...and say unto Zion, Thou art my people."* Clearly this passage is referencing God's dealings with Israel *in the future*.

Wait just a cotton-pickin' minute, as an entertainer of a previous generation used to say. If, as replacement theology maintains, God has replaced the Jews with the Church, why do we see so much language regarding the Jews and the nation of Israel (Zion) in prophetic literature? Why talk about the future of Israel if they were not even going to exist? That doesn't make any sense at all!

The Timeline of Prophecy

There is no question that these prophecies are dealing with future events. In addition, Zion is regarded in these passages in contrast to the Gentiles, referring to the nations around Israel. Those nations and Israel are obviously separate and distinct in the mind of God as He inspired His prophets to speak.

How can anyone honestly say that the Jews are unnecessary? God obviously has them in mind when it comes to future events. In fact, as we will see, God will deal with Israel almost exclusively in end-time events. It is in the land of Israel that most of end-time prophecy unfolds.

Before I get to the language included in the book of Revelation, I want to refer to a unique and specific timeline given to the prophet Daniel by none other than a special emissary from Heaven, the angel Gabriel. Daniel 9:24-27 says:

> Seventy weeks are determined upon thy people and upon thy holy city, to finish the transgression, and to make an end of sins, and to make reconciliation for iniquity, and to bring in everlasting righteousness, and to seal up the vision and prophecy, and to anoint the most Holy.
>
> Know therefore and understand, that from the going forth of the commandment to restore and to

> build Jerusalem unto the Messiah the Prince shall be seven weeks, and threescore and two weeks: the street shall be built again, and the wall, even in troublous times.
>
> And after threescore and two weeks shall Messiah be cut off, but not for himself: and the people of the prince that shall come shall destroy the city and the sanctuary; and the end thereof shall be with a flood, and unto the end of the war desolations are determined.
>
> And ***he shall confirm the covenant*** with many for one week: and in the midst of the week he shall cause the sacrifice and the oblation to cease, and for the overspreading of abominations he shall make it desolate, even until the consummation, and that determined shall be poured upon the desolate.

Let me briefly unpack some of this passage, at least as much as refers to Israel and the end times. The term *weeks* as it is used here is *sevens*. It is generally understood to mean seven years. Therefore, 70 weeks is 490 years.

Keep in mind throughout this discussion that Gabriel is addressing Daniel, who is a Jew, and his people are Jews. Something significant is going to happen regarding the Jews involving 490 years. Some say this period of time is over, since we are much more than 490 years removed from Daniel's day.

However, what Gabriel is saying cannot be explained in linear arithmetic.

We have several markers to help guide us about this passage. The first one is regarding the commandment to restore and build Jerusalem.

This decree was issued in 454 BC (see Nehemiah 2:1-8). (The dates I am using may be different at the front and back end by a year or so, but the time interval between them is not.)

- Seven sevens of years later, or 49 years, Jerusalem was rebuilt.
- 62 weeks of years, or 434 years after Jerusalem was rebuilt, Jesus was crucified outside the gates of the city.
- 49 years plus 434 years equals 483 years, or 69 weeks of years (69 x 7 = 483).
- That ended this segment of time.

The following is a suggested timeline of these events:

- 454 BC minus 49 years = 405 BC
- 405 BC minus 400 years = 5 BC (the so-called silent years between Malachi and Matthew)
- 5 BC plus 34 years of Jesus' lifetime on earth = AD 29 when Jesus was crucified *("...cut off, but not for Himself...."* as Gabriel said to Daniel)
- Total = 483 years

As you can see, there are seven years remaining to make up the 490 years that Gabriel mentioned to Daniel. What period of time will result in 7 years of God dealing with Israel? I believe that it refers to the time known as the Tribulation period.

In the Daniel passage, the *"people of the prince that shall come"* refers to the Romans. They destroyed the city of Jerusalem and the temple under Titus in AD 70.

The Revealing of the Antichrist

The next *"he"* referred to in this passage does not refer to a Roman legionnaire of the 1st century. This will be a different leader of what many believe will be a coalition of nations representing what is essentially a revived Roman empire. This leader's behavior reveals his identity. Among his other actions, he will:

- ***Confirm a covenant*** with many for one week (seven years). This is a covenant of peace with Israel, and marks the 70th seven-year period of 70-week or 490-year time frame mentioned in Daniel.
- ***Violate the covenant*** halfway through this seven-year period, causing the sacrifices being made in the rebuilt temple to cease.
- ***Do something that is abominable to the Jews***, calling to remembrance the abomination of desolation accomplished by Antiochus Epiphanes centuries before.

- ***Ultimately be defeated.*** This is none other than the antichrist, who is revealed in Revelation 6:2:

> And I saw, and behold a white horse: and he that sat on him had a bow; and a crown was given unto him: and he went forth conquering, and to conquer.

The antichrist will rise to power as the result of satan's influence (see Revelation 13:2). The first half of his seven-year reign will be marked by flattery, diplomacy, and treachery. He will not reveal his violent and deadly aims at first. He will attempt to get what he wants by means of deception and manipulation. Only when those tactics no longer fulfill his purposes will he resort to violence and repression.

Many say the antichrist's aim will be world domination, but that will only be a secondary goal. His primary purpose will be singular and relentless. *The reason he arises is to destroy the nation of Israel, and to annihilate every Jew on the face of the earth.*

You may remember that I outlined several episodes in Israel's history that were designed by their adversaries to kill them all. The antichrist will make all their efforts, as devastating as they were, look like children stepping on ants at a picnic. The antichrist will combine military might, economic power, media control, and social influence to identify, isolate, and immolate every Jew he can locate.

Jesus Discusses the End Times with His Followers

Jesus spoke to His followers about these events, recorded in Matthew chapter 24. Let's take a brief look at what Jesus says in Matthew 24:3:

> And as he sat upon the mount of Olives, the disciples came unto him privately, saying, Tell us, when shall these things be? and what shall be the sign of thy coming, and of the end of the world?

We can summarize Jesus' answer as follows:

- Imposters will arise claiming to be Christ.
- You will hear of wars and rumors of wars.
- Famines, pestilence, and earthquakes will become common.
- Persecution will increase in frequency and severity.
- Betrayal and hatred will become common.
- False prophets will proliferate.
- Iniquity and apostasy will abound.
- The gospel will be preached to all nations before the end comes.

So far, we can legitimately say that the conditions Jesus is describing here could refer to either the present age or the first half of what is known as the Tribulation period. However, what comes next is certainly referring to the flash point that will kick off the second half of that seven-year period. The text continues with verses 15-30.

To summarize that passage, I offer these points:

- Jesus refers to the abomination of desolation described in Daniel 9:27. This is an unmistakable signal to every Jew living in Israel or in that entire region to flee. Where are they supposed to go? Very likely to Moab, Ammon, and Edom, according to Revelation 12:14.
- The warning is definite: run for your lives, and don't turn back to try to take anything with you.
- Whatever persecution the Jews have endured up to now is about to be multiplied. It will be a time of great tribulation, not only for Jews, but especially for them.
- False prophets working deceptive signs and wonders will abound, and will try to trick people into revealing their whereabouts to meet those who pretend to be the Messiah. In order to stay safe, those in hiding must not believe the lies.
- Christ's coming will be unmistakable. No lying sign or wonder will be able to mimic His appearing. Revelation 19:11-16 tells it this way:

> And I saw heaven opened, and behold a white horse; and he that sat upon him was called Faithful and True, and in righteousness he doth judge and make war. His eyes were as a flame of fire, and on his head were many crowns; and he had a name written, that no man knew, but he himself. And he was clothed with a vesture dipped in blood: and his name is called The Word of God. And the armies which were in heaven followed him upon white horses, clothed in fine linen, white and clean. And out of his mouth goeth a sharp sword, that with it he should smite the nations: and he shall rule them with a rod of iron: and he treadeth the winepress of the fierceness and wrath of Almighty God. And he hath on his vesture and on his thigh a name written, King Of Kings, And Lord Of Lords.

- The mention of the carcass and the vultures refers to this activity centering on Israel, and especially Jerusalem.
- The tribes (nations or peoples) of the earth shall mourn—this refers to unbelievers, whose righteous judgment is at hand.

The 144,000, the Woman, and the Man Child

Another truth that proves that the Jews figure prominently in God's plan for the end times is found in Revelation 7:3-4:

> Saying, Hurt not the earth, neither the sea, nor the trees, till we have sealed the servants of our God in their foreheads. And I heard the number of them which were sealed: and there were sealed an hundred and forty and four thousand of all the tribes of the children of Israel.

Twelve thousand from each of the 12 tribes of Israel receive a mark of divine protection. Their purpose is not specifically mentioned, but the next scene is of a great multitude of the righteous standing before the throne of God, praising Him.

One of the elders around the throne tells John that this multitude represents those who have received salvation during the tribulation period. Perhaps the job of these thousands of Jews who are sealed is to preach the gospel to the nations during the first half of the tribulation period. If that is the case, they have obviously had great success.

One more thing that indicates the centrality of Israel in end-time events is in Revelation 12:1-6:

> And there appeared a great wonder in heaven; a woman clothed with the sun, and the moon under her feet, and upon her head a crown of twelve stars: And she being with child cried, travailing in birth, and pained to be delivered.

> And there appeared another wonder in heaven; and behold a great red dragon, having seven heads and ten horns, and seven crowns upon his heads. And his tail drew the third part of the stars of heaven, and did cast them to the earth: and the dragon stood before the woman which was ready to be delivered, for to devour her child as soon as it was born.
>
> And she brought forth a man child, who was to rule all nations with a rod of iron: and her child was caught up unto God, and to his throne. And the woman fled into the wilderness, where she hath a place prepared of God, that they should feed her there a thousand two hundred and threescore days [three and a half years].

The woman is Israel, the dragon is satan, and the man child is the Lord Jesus Christ. Additional details about the woman are in Revelation 12:13-17:

> And when the dragon saw that he was cast unto the earth, he persecuted the woman which brought forth the man child. And to the woman were given two wings of a great eagle, that she might fly into the wilderness, into her place, where she is nourished for a time, and times, and half a time, from the face of the serpent.

> And the serpent cast out of his mouth water as a flood after the woman, that he might cause her to be carried away of the flood. And the earth helped the woman, and the earth opened her mouth, and swallowed up the flood which the dragon cast out of his mouth.
>
> And the dragon was wroth with the woman, and went to make war with the remnant of her seed, which keep the commandments of God, and have the testimony of Jesus Christ.

There are more Scripture passages than I have space to mention that make it clear that Israel and the Jews are not only included, but they are also central to the drama that will take place at the end of the age.

Replacement theology denies this and attempts to spiritualize and neutralize these Scripture passages and many others like them. The proponents of replacement theology need to *replace their theology* rather than replacing the clear intent of the Word of God regarding Israel and the Jews.

LIE #6

THE LIE OF THE DISCONNECTED ROOT

As we have already seen, the Abrahamic covenant involves his descendants being a blessing to all the nations of the earth. The epitome of that blessing was bringing the Lord Jesus Christ to the earth. Since that blessing has already been accomplished, the proponents of replacement theology maintain that the Jews have no further significance. That is a wrong conclusion for several reasons. Let's examine the lie that says Israel is spiritually irrelevant to the Church.

Significance and Purpose

What if someone decided that you had no further significance, that your purpose in life had been fulfilled, and that you could not justify taking up space on earth any longer? Would it surprise you to know that there is a growing contingent of people who still make those exact claims about certain groups of people?

They use terms such as "useless eater" (this was commonly used by the Nazis, by the way), "nonproductive, a drain on society," and other pejorative labels.

Here is good news. Our significance does not and cannot come from other people. Certainly, we all want to be validated by and have the approval of other people. However, our significance as human beings can only come from God. In addition, our sense of purpose ultimately comes from God—not from anyone or anything else.

Here is more good news. Individuals and nations can and do have more than one purpose in their existence. Without doubt, the Jewish people existed to create a nation from whom the Messiah would come.

God's Representatives on Earth

However, it is naïve to think that was their only purpose. Another purpose for Israel, both ancient and modern, is that they represent God on earth, at all times and to all nations. They have always been and continue to be God's "peculiar treasure." I didn't coin this phrase. God Himself did. Exodus 19:3-6 says:

> And Moses went up unto God, and the Lord called unto him out of the mountain, saying, Thus shalt thou say to the house of Jacob, and tell the children of Israel; Ye have seen what I did unto the Egyptians, and how I bare you on eagles' wings, and brought you unto myself.
>
> Now therefore, if ye will obey my voice indeed, and keep my covenant, then ***ye shall be a peculiar treasure unto me above all people***: for all the earth is mine: And ye shall be unto me a kingdom of priests, and an holy nation. These are the words which thou shalt speak unto the children of Israel.

Let everything be confirmed by two or three witnesses. Here is a second witness: As long as Jews remain, people have an unalterable witness of the faithfulness of God. They are special because God chose them, not because of any innate qualities they have. Deuteronomy 7:6-10 reads:

> For thou art an holy people unto the Lord thy God: the Lord thy God hath chosen thee to be a special people unto himself, above all people that are upon the face of the earth. The Lord did not set his love upon you, nor choose you, because ye were more in number than any people; for ye were the fewest of all people:

> But because ***the Lord loved you***, and ***because he would keep the oath*** which he had sworn unto your fathers, hath the Lord brought you out with a mighty hand, and redeemed you out of the house of bondmen, from the hand of Pharaoh king of Egypt.
>
> Know therefore that the Lord thy God, he is God, the faithful God, which keepeth covenant and mercy with them that love him and keep his commandments to a thousand generations; and repayeth them that hate him to their face, to destroy them: he will not be slack to him that hateth him, he will repay him to his face.

And a third witness:

> Only the Lord had a delight in thy fathers to love them, and ***he chose their seed*** after them, even you above all people, as it is this day (Deuteronomy 10:15).

That is why the devil hates the Jews (and Christians, too) and wants more than anything to destroy them; he knows that they represent God on earth. This has nothing to do with whether Jews believe in Christ as Savior or not—it is the very fact that they are descendants of Abraham and are alive on earth. This represents God's faithfulness and immutability.

You are special, also, because God chose you—not because of any innate qualities you have. The Bible declares a humbling truth in Romans 5:8: *"while we were yet sinners, Christ died for us."*

The initiative was God's. This does not mean that some people are excluded. The Bible makes it clear that God is merciful to all, and His desire is that none would perish, but that *all* would come to repentance (see 2 Peter 3:9).

Touch Not God's Anointed

In Psalm 105:6-15, King David is rehearsing the dealings of God with His people. No one can argue the fact that the Jews were, and are, God's chosen people, set apart for His own purpose. Another way of stating this is to say that they were *anointed* by God.

The Hebrew word *mashiach,* meaning anointed one, is used in verse 15. It comes from the word *masach,* which means to pour or rub oil on someone to indicate that they have been set apart for a special purpose. Here is the passage:

> O ye seed of Abraham his servant, ye children of Jacob his chosen. He is the Lord our God: his judgments are in all the earth. He hath remembered his covenant for ever, the word which he commanded to a ***thousand generations.***

> Which covenant he made with Abraham, and his oath unto Isaac; And confirmed the same unto Jacob for a law, and to Israel for an ***everlasting covenant***: Saying, Unto thee will I give the land of Canaan, the lot of your inheritance: When they were but a few men in number; yea, very few, and strangers in it.
>
> When they went from one nation to another, from one kingdom to another people; He ***suffered no man to do them wrong***: yea, he reproved kings for their sakes; saying, ***Touch not mine anointed***, and do my prophets no harm (Psalm 105:6-15).

Let's review a few important thoughts from these verses. This same passage is repeated almost verbatim in 1 Chronicles 16:13-22. The fact that it was repeated signifies its importance, and tells us to take note of it.

"To a thousand generations." Whenever we see this phrase used in the Bible, we need to understand that this was an expression that signified an *everlasting covenant*—in other words: *forever.* David is rehearsing the covenant that God made with His people.

He goes on to talk about Israel's long history of conquering and being conquered. I don't know of another nation as small that has triumphed over as much adversity. There may be one, but I don't know of it. In any case, the fact they still exist as a people and a nation is a bona fide miracle!

"He suffered no man to do them wrong." Look at the nations and leaders of nations throughout history that have come against Israel or the Jews. Though they may have defeated Israel in the short term, look at their continued history. You could easily come to the same conclusion I did: God always vindicates His chosen people.

"Touch not mine anointed." The context of Psalm 105 and 1 Chronicles 16 makes King David's meaning clear when he says, *"touch not mine anointed and do my prophets no harm."* It is not directed at preachers, as it is often used today. It is clear that King David is referring to the patriarchs of old (he mentions Abraham, Isaac, and Jacob), and by extension, the nation of Israel (the Jews) that sprang from them.

The caution is there twice in the Bible, emphasizing the importance of not speaking or acting against the nation of Israel, God's chosen people.

Today's preachers who take this phrase out of context and use it to stop people from talking about them (and their indiscretions) and to shield themselves from criticism are not to be compared to the patriarchs of old who fathered or led nations!

This understanding underscores that God's admonition to honor His anointed was directed toward the patriarchs and the nation of Israel, reinforcing the biblical foundation for Israel's enduring significance and directly challenging the claims of replacement theology.

Targeted for Destruction

Jews, in a way, are the proverbial canary in the coal mine. What happens to them is not limited to them and will eventually spread to other people groups. In Hitler's Germany, Jews were not the only people who were targeted for persecution and destruction.

Lest we forget the faithful who came before us, we need to understand that Christians (also chosen by God) have been on the enemy's radar for millennia.

Christians have been martyred for their faith, ostracized for their faith, criticized for their faith, and shamed for their faith. Jesus makes the reason clear in John 15:19: "*... because ye are not of the world, but I have chosen you out of the world, therefore the world hateth you.*"

The enemy's hatred for God is the fuel that drives the world's desire to destroy whomever God loves.

Here is a list of some other groups considered subhuman or inferior in some way, and who were also killed en masse by the Nazis:

- Roma (also known as gypsies)—up to 500,000 killed
- People with disabilities—up to 250,000 killed
- Poles and other Slavs—millions killed
- Russian prisoners of war—over 3 million killed
- Blacks
- Political opponents
- Religious leaders who resisted Nazi policies

Speaking of religious leaders, there were those who resisted Nazi policies. Perhaps the best known of these was Dietrich Bonhoeffer, who became involved in a plot to assassinate Hitler. He was arrested and executed shortly before the end of World War II.

One of his colleagues, Martin Niemöller, was a supporter of Hitler at first. Niemöller was a proponent of the idea that the reason the Jews had suffered such persecution was because they were responsible for crucifying Jesus Christ.

Niemöller later began to speak out against the Nazi regime and was subsequently sent to the concentration camps, somehow surviving until the end of the war. He was liberated by Allied soldiers.

After the war, Niemöller was famously (and often) quoted as being repentant that he and many others did not speak up for the persecuted minorities. By the time he was arrested, he said, there was nobody left to speak up on his behalf. These remarks were originally made in a speech at the Confessing Church in Frankfurt, Germany, in 1946.

How It Starts

Churches in Germany during the Nazi regime generally held one of three positions. First: a very few openly resisted Nazi policies. Second: most churches were silent, fearing criticism, confiscation, or closure. Third: some were either enthusiastic supporters of Nazi aims, or they willingly collaborated with the Nazis.

You may rightly ask how a church filled with believers in Jesus Christ could accommodate such a position as the antisemitism that was a cornerstone of Nazi policy. One reason it happened is that many in those churches had already been steeped in antisemitic rhetoric and had already developed a long-standing cultural bias against Jews. This is not surprising, since as we have already seen, Martin Luther first disseminated his hateful antisemitic discourses across Germany.

I am concerned that the same atmosphere is beginning to form in the United States and elsewhere in the world due to the faulty theology of *supersessionism*. It may not be a confirmed point of view in the minds of some who are talking about it. However, we must consider how these ideas move from the fringes of cultural consciousness to mainstream thinking.

One way this happens is through the prevalence of social media. Many people have access to ways of making their opinions known that were unavailable in ages past. A generation ago, a mere letter to the editor of a newspaper had to make it past editorial review before it could be published. Today, anyone can say just about anything about anything or anybody, regardless of how outlandish or unsupported it may be.

Once it is out there in the ether, it can be seen, heard, and repeated by anyone. In some cases, the more sensational the idea (or at least the headline), the more likely it is to be viewed or repeated. This creates a cycle of more and more bizarre claims, and there is no way to stop the discussion once it begins. This is how the most extreme claims gain traction, even though they may have no connection to reality.

Here is a corollary to that thought. Sometimes people will promote an idea that they know is far beyond the boundaries of good sense or common decency. Their goal is not to say something they firmly believe. What they want to gauge is how much resistance to their idea they have coming back at them.

If the response is uniformly and overwhelmingly negative, they put that idea on the shelf, perhaps to be recycled later. If the opposition is only tepid, or if there is no response at all, they take that as a signal that there are other people who will agree with them.

They believe the lack of pushback is tacit approval that their idea will be received by others, even if they may not be openly enthusiastic about it at first. In some cases, this procedure is how yesterday's crazy theories can become tomorrow's headlines.

The reason I am so adamant about resisting replacement theology is not that it has already captured the minds and hearts of many thought leaders in Christianity. My concern is that if we do not firmly and thoroughly repudiate replacement theology now, it has the potential to become a dominant position in the thinking of many more people than it already has.

The slippery slope will become steeper and more slippery. First, it will be the Jews. Then it will be some other group. Then it will be you and me—and by that time, there will be nobody left to object to our being marginalized, then ostracized, and then…replaced.

They Blamed the Jews for Killing Jesus

I need to circle back to something I mentioned in Chapter 1 and that I also referred to when discussing Martin Niemöller: Jews being persecuted because of their complicity in the death of Jesus.

The issue of the Jews being responsible for *deicide* (the term literally means "the killing of a god") needs to be put to rest permanently.

Jesus of Nazareth created a problem for the *Jewish religious leaders in Jerusalem*—several problems, in fact. One was that He repeatedly pointed out their incandescent hypocrisy and their refusal to abide by the law of Moses.

The Jewish leaders loved the chief seats at feasts. They loved to be called *rabbi, master,* or *father*. They loved to make a public show of their loud prayers and generous giving. They loved to be the final arbiters in matters of right and wrong. They loved to accuse others of error while excusing their own errors.

They would resort to lies, deceit, and treachery to maintain their positions of power and influence. They would go to any length to remove anyone they saw as a threat to their authority. Most of the conflicts that Jesus encountered during His earthly ministry were with the religious leaders.

Another problem that Jesus posed to the ruling elite was that He was becoming increasingly popular, and they were becoming increasingly unpopular. Something had to be done. It seems that the resurrection of Lazarus crystallized their opposition. They desperately searched for a way they could credibly get rid of this Teacher from Galilee.

A third difficulty was that Jesus was attracting the attention of the governing authorities. The wife of Herod's steward was one of His supporters (see Luke 8:3). Consider this passage about conditions after Lazarus was raised from the dead, from John 11:46-53:

But some of them went their ways to the Pharisees, and told them what things Jesus had done. Then gathered the chief priests and the Pharisees a council, and said, What do we? for this man doeth many miracles. If we let him thus alone, all men will believe on him: and the Romans shall come and take away both ***our place and nation***.

And one of them, named Caiaphas, being the high priest that same year, said unto them, Ye know nothing at all, nor consider that it is expedient for us, that one man should die for the people, and that the whole nation perish not.

And this spake he not of himself: but being high priest that year, he prophesied that Jesus should die for that nation; and not for that nation only, but that also he should gather together in one the children of God that were scattered abroad. Then from that day forth they took counsel together for to put him to death.

Here is their line of thinking:

He makes us look bad.
He exposes our inconsistencies.
He threatens our way of life.
He puts us all at risk.
Therefore, we must get rid of Him.

This created two problems for the Jewish leaders: First, they could not find a way to get rid of Jesus, since the crowds all wanted to hear what He had to say. To arrest Him in the middle of such a gathering would risk mob violence against anyone who would attempt to harm Him.

Second, the Romans reserved the legal authority to put someone to death. However, there were times when they ignored that law, and either tolerated or allowed the Jews to execute someone (see Acts 7:59-60).

In the case of Jesus of Nazareth, it became a political powder keg for Pontius Pilate, and he is the one who finally sentenced Jesus to death on the Cross. It is true that Jesus was declared guilty of blasphemy by the Jewish council, which was a capital offense.

However, Jesus was scourged by Romans, mocked and abused by Romans (along with Herod and his courtiers), sentenced by the Roman governor, and crucified by Romans. Did the Jews share responsibility for what happened to Jesus? Jesus indicated that at least one of them did in John 19:11:

> Jesus answered, Thou couldest have no power at all against me, except it were given thee from above: therefore he that delivered me unto thee hath the greater sin.

That person was Judas, the betrayer. Read these chilling words from Matthew 27:24-25:

> When Pilate saw that he could prevail nothing, but that rather a tumult was made, he took water, and washed his hands before the multitude, saying, I am innocent of the blood of this just person: see ye to it. Then answered all the people, and said, His blood be on us, and on our children.

About 40 years later, the traditional length of a generation, both the temple and the city were destroyed by the Romans. Caiphas had fretted that the Romans would take away the Jews' *place* (the temple and the city of Jerusalem) and their *nation* (the Jews in Judea) if Jesus did not die. Jesus was crucified, and the Romans took away both their place and their nation anyway.

Jesus Laid Down His Life

Were the Jews, or at least the Jewish religious rulers, involved in the death of Jesus of Nazareth? The Bible record makes it clear that they were. Were they solely and ultimately responsible for His death? Absolutely and conclusively not! Here is why I can say that with such conviction.

First, Jesus understood from the very beginning of His ministry that His purpose was to die on a cross. Later, He told His disciples that this would be the outcome (see Mark 8:31). No less than a sacrificial lamb brought to Jerusalem by a sincere pilgrim at Passover, Jesus knew that He was born to die. Next, Jesus also says in John 10:17-18:

> Therefore doth my Father love me, because I lay down my life, that I might take it again. ***No man taketh it from me, but I lay it down of myself.*** I have power to lay it down, and I have power to take it again. This commandment have I received of my Father.

When Peter tried to defend Jesus from arrest in the garden of Gethsemane, Jesus says in Matthew 26:53-54:

> Thinkest thou that I cannot now pray to my Father, and he shall presently give me more than twelve legions of angels? But how then shall the scriptures be fulfilled, that thus it must be?

Jesus gave His life willingly. Hear the prophet's testimony from Isaiah 53:7:

> He was oppressed, and he was afflicted, yet he opened not his mouth: he is brought as a lamb to the slaughter, and as a sheep before her shearers is dumb, so he openeth not his mouth.

The author of Hebrews applies this passage specifically to the Messiah (see Hebrews 10:5-10). Psalm 40:7-8 says:

> Then said I, Lo, I come: in the volume of the book it is written of me, I delight to do thy will, O my God: yea, thy law is within my heart.

Finally, Jesus did not die for only one people group. One man's sins, or one nation's sins, were not solely responsible for His death. All of us were guilty before God, and all of us participated in His condemnation and crucifixion.

We were not there among that mob in front of Pilate in Jerusalem that day, but if we had been, we, too, would have demanded His death. Romans 11:32 says:

> For God hath concluded them ***all*** in unbelief, that he might have mercy upon all.

This leads us to a very important point of discussion: how do the Jews figure in the plan of redemption, and where does that leave us today?

The apostle Paul has a great deal more to say about this in Romans 11. In the upcoming final chapter, we will take a look at his remarks and what they mean to both us and the Jewish people.

LIE #7

THE LIE OF THE CLOSED BOOK

Paul settles this lie. In Romans 11, the apostle gives one of the clearest, most direct statements in all of Scripture about Israel's future; and yet proponents of replacement theology routinely sidestep it, insisting that the restoration prophecies Paul describes have already been fulfilled.

They prefer a different passage. Galatians 3:28 has become their go-to proof text:

> There is neither Jew nor Greek, there is neither bond nor free, there is neither male nor female: for ye are all one in Christ Jesus.

In a classic case of taking a Scripture verse out of context to try to prove a point, the supersessionists say that this proves that God does not make a distinction between Jews and Gentiles any longer. This is a lie.

The point Paul is making in this chapter, and indeed in the entire book of Galatians, is that it is impossible for anyone to be justified before God by attempting to fulfill the requirements of the law of Moses.

The only way anyone can be justified before God is through faith in Jesus Christ as Savior. This is true whether you are a Jew, a Gentile, or whether you claim any other distinction that it is possible to claim. The requirements are the same for everyone, regardless of who they are, from whence they came, or what their history has been.

Jews do not lose their distinction as Jews because of faith in Christ, nor did God intend them to. Here is the proof—the same Scripture verse that says there is neither Jew nor Greek also says there is neither male nor female.

Paul is not trying to prove that men and women lose their distinctiveness or their identity because of faith in Jesus. The very notion is ridiculous. Paul is clearly saying that there is no difference in what a man must do and what a woman must do to be saved.

He is also saying that nobody has an advantage over anyone else in the Church—all believers have a personal relationship with the Lord Jesus Christ on the basis of faith.

This refusal to accept common sense is on full display in many places in our culture. God has always intended that men and women are equal in His sight. He emphatically did not intend for them to be the same.

There are those who will not admit that there are any differences between men and women. They do their best to blur the lines of what is basic biology and human history. They turn reason and observation on their heads in a futile attempt to move an unreasonable and ungodly doctrine forward. The result of these efforts is not empathy and compassion, but confusion and chaos.

As we have already seen, God is not the author of confusion; rather, He brings order to chaos. I want to deal with how He does that to the issue of replacement theology in the pages ahead.

The Proof Is in the Parable?

Supersessionists are also fond of using the following parable to prove their point. The context is Jesus again contending with the Pharisees, shortly after His entry into Jerusalem. It is found in Matthew 21:33-43:

> Hear another parable: There was a certain householder, which planted a vineyard, and hedged it round about, and digged a winepress in it, and built

a tower, and let it out to husbandmen, and went into a far country: And when the time of the fruit drew near, he sent his servants to the husbandmen, that they might receive the fruits of it.

And the husbandmen took his servants, and beat one, and killed another, and stoned another. Again, he sent other servants more than the first: and they did unto them likewise. But last of all he sent unto them his son, saying, They will reverence my son. But when the husbandmen saw the son, they said among themselves, This is the heir; come, let us kill him, and let us seize on his inheritance. And they caught him, cast him out of the vineyard, and slew him.

When the lord therefore of the vineyard cometh, what will he do unto those husbandmen? They say unto him, He will miserably destroy those wicked men, and will let out his vineyard unto other husbandmen, which shall render him the fruits in their seasons. Jesus saith unto them, Did ye never read in the scriptures, The stone which the builders rejected, the same is become the head of the corner: this is the Lord's doing, and it is marvellous in our eyes? Therefore say I unto you, The kingdom of God shall be taken from you, and given to a nation bringing forth the fruits thereof.

The supersessionists say this parable proves that God is finished with the Jews and has given the Kingdom of God to the Gentiles. While it is certainly true that God has opened the door of salvation to the Gentiles, which has always been His plan, He has by no means excluded the Jews from His oversight and offer of salvation.

Just because God accepted the Gentiles does not mean that He has rejected the Jews. There is room in God's Kingdom for everyone, and the means of access is the same for everyone—*faith in Jesus Christ.*

You may recognize that I am repeating this theme. Rest assured it bears repeating—indeed, it cannot be emphasized enough. Jesus says in John 14:6:

> I am the way, the truth, and the life: no man cometh unto the Father, but by me.

Are the Jews In or Out?

It does not matter to what people group you belong, how many religious works you have done, or how many of your ancestors have been churchgoers. The only thing that matters in eternity is whether you have put your faith and trust in Jesus Christ as your Savior.

Romans chapter 11 puts the entire supersessionism issue in proper perspective. I want to include a portion of it here, from The Message version of the Bible. I encourage you to read Romans 11 in its entirety.

As you do, I am confident that it will help clear up many of the misconceptions and assumptions that have been made by replacement theology. I will summarize certain portions of the chapter, and also include comments that I trust will be helpful to you as you go through it.

Before we begin discussing Romans 11, I want to include some background that gives context about why the book of Romans was written.

As we see from Acts 2, Jews from all over the Roman Empire were present in Jerusalem on the day of Pentecost. No doubt some from Rome were there, since there had been a Jewish presence in Rome for some time. It is likely that some of these visitors saw and experienced the outpouring of the Holy Spirit. They returned to Rome, and naturally, a church began there.

As time went on and the church began to grow, conflict between orthodox Jews and Messianic Jews was inevitable. This conflict devolved into riots, causing an uproar in the city and no small concern for the authorities. The Romans dealt with the problem by banishing all the Jews from Rome. This resulted in the leaders of the church in Rome (who were Jews) moving away.

Eventually, the church in Rome was reestablished, but this time it was made up of Gentiles. Once again, the church began to grow. The current Roman emperor then decided that the Jews could be allowed back into the city.

The opportunity for the Jews to return to Rome meant that some of the same Jews who had become believers in Jesus returned and began to fellowship in the church at Rome.

As you can imagine, it was awkward at best for those Jewish believers who had been involved in leadership positions in the church to see their places taken by Gentiles.

One of the reasons the apostle Paul wrote to the church at Rome was to deal with the difficulties that Jewish believers and Gentile believers experienced as they worshiped together in the same church. That is why Paul spent so much time and gave so much emphasis to the concept of Jews and Gentiles being part of the same body.

It is also why the book of Romans, and especially Romans chapter 11, is so helpful to us in understanding what God has in mind for both the Jews and the Gentiles in these last days.

Romans 11:1-2 (MSG) says:

> Does this mean, then, that God is so fed up with Israel that he'll have nothing more to do with them? Hardly. Remember that I, the one writing these things, am an Israelite, a descendant of Abraham out of the tribe of Benjamin. You can't get much more Semitic than that! So we're not talking about repudiation. God has been

> too long involved with Israel, has too much invested, to simply wash his hands of them.

I could stop here and consider these verses to be a full and final answer to replacement theology. However, Paul has much more to say along this line.

After Elijah's showdown with the prophets of Baal in 1 Kings 18, he cried out to God because he felt alone and abandoned. His plea and God's response is in 1 Kings 19:13-18. Paul reiterates this in Romans 11:3-6 (MSG):

> Do you remember that time Elijah was agonizing over this same Israel and cried out in prayer? God, they murdered your prophets, they trashed your altars; I'm the only one left and now they're after me!
>
> And do you remember God's answer? I still have seven thousand who haven't quit, Seven thousand who are loyal to the finish. It's the same today. There's a fiercely loyal minority still—not many, perhaps, but probably more than you think. They're holding on, not because of what they think they're going to get out of it, but because they're convinced of God's grace and purpose in choosing them.

You may think you are alone and abandoned, but God knows those who belong to Him. These faithful followers are not remaining in faith for what they think they stand to benefit from it.

They are doing what they do for Him and Him alone.

Let's look at some of the notable Jews who believed in Jesus during His life and ministry and beyond:

- In Luke 8, Jairus, a ruler of a synagogue, besought Jesus to come and heal his daughter—and Jesus did.
- John 12:42 says that many of the chief rulers of the Jews believed in Jesus.
- At least one member of the ruling council, Nicodemus, did as well.
- Joseph of Arimathea, a wealthy man, was also a disciple.
- Many Jewish priests became believers in Jesus (see Acts 6:7).
- Acts 18:8 says that the chief ruler of the synagogue in Corinth believed in Jesus, along with all his family.

So we see a remnant of Jews who believed in Jesus even before the crucifixion, and certainly afterward.

Self-Interest, or God-Interest?

Romans 11:7 (MSG) continues:

> And then what happened? Well, when Israel tried to be right with God on her own, pursuing her own

self-interest, she didn't succeed. The chosen ones of God were those who let God pursue his interest in them, and as a result received his stamp of legitimacy. The "self-interest Israel" became thick-skinned toward God.

The next verse, Romans 11:8, says that God gave the unbelieving ones a spirit of slumber, with eyes that cannot see and ears that cannot hear.

There are consequences to disobedience. Blurred eyes and dull ears are some of those consequences. Some people are indignant that God would give people a spirit of slumber. What else would He do to those who revel in their unbelief? Not only are those unbelievers unrepentant, but they are also actually proud of their disbelief and disobedience.

It is one thing to sleep in the dark. It is another thing altogether to sleep in bright sunshine. Ephesians 5:14 says, *"Wherefore he saith, Awake thou that sleepest, and arise from the dead, and Christ shall give thee light."*

Romans 11:11-15 continues making the contrast between the unbelieving Jews and the faithful Gentiles, and the reason for this seeming discrepancy:

- The Jews walked out, and the Gentiles walked in.
- Perhaps the Jews will see what the Gentiles have obtained and wonder what they are missing out on.

- Their leaving triggered a multitude of Gentiles to come into the Kingdom of God.
- Their return will be even more monumental.
- Paul said he emphasizes what the Gentiles have gained when talking to Jews—his purpose is to provoke the Jews to find out what is available to them through faith in Jesus.
- Paul says it again—the Jews fell away, and the Gentiles fell in—think about what will happen when the Jews fall in, too.

It was never God's intention to exclude the nations of the world from salvation. However, it was only right for Him to offer it to His people first. When they rejected it, it did not mean that He could not offer it to others. God has had this in mind from the very beginning.

Pruning and Grafting Branches

In Romans 11:11-15, Paul uses a concept that was familiar to those in the ancient world—dealing with grafting trees. Grafting is a process that involves attaching branches from a different plant to existing rootstock. The intended result is to get the best characteristics of both plants in one tree.

So it is with the Jews and the Gentiles. God plans for both of them to make up one body of believers, not losing their distinctions, but allowing those distinctions to add uniqueness and completeness to the body of Christ.

- God started with a holy root: if the root is holy, the fruit will be holy.
- The Gentiles were like wild olive tree branches grafted to that holy root.
- Some of the tree's original branches had to be pruned off to allow Gentiles to be grafted in. The Gentiles should not boast about this, since the root feeds the branch, and not the other way around.
- The reason branches were pruned so Gentiles could be included was because of the original branches' unbelief.
- Gentiles need to remember that the reason they are included is because of faith in Christ.
- God pruned the original branches to make room for you—don't you think He could and would prune your branches to make room for others if you fall into disbelief?
- God is good, but He is also just. He is good to all, but He will not hesitate to prune out dead and unprofitable wood to make room for more fruit.
- Don't feel superior to the branches that were pruned—you have what you have because of God's grace, not your own merit.
- If God pruned branches off, He can graft them in again.
- He grafted you in from a wild olive tree—how much more can He reattach branches from the original tree?

God's Oldest Friends

Romans 11:25-27 further deals with God's purpose in all this.

- Paul calls this a mystery.
- Part of the reason for the blindness of the Jews is so that the harvest of Gentiles can be completed.
- Israel's day is coming—and their Redeemer is coming to forgive their sins just as He forgave ours.

The Message Bible goes on to say, in Romans 11:28-29:

> From your point of view as you hear and embrace the good news of the Message, it looks like the Jews are God's enemies. But looked at from the long-range perspective of God's overall purpose, they remain God's oldest friends. God's gifts and God's call are under full warranty—never canceled, never rescinded.

God always has a different perspective, as He sits on the circle of eternity, beyond the bounds of time and space. Let us pray that we get a glimpse of things the way He sees them. We see partially and imperfectly, but even a partial or obscured view is far better than the blindness we experienced before we came to faith in Christ Jesus.

God's Covenants Are Eternal

In Romans 11:30-36, Paul concludes his masterful explanation of the relationship between Jews and Gentiles in making up the complete body of Christ.

- Not so long ago, Gentiles were outside of God's covenant. They received God's mercy as a result of the unbelief of others.
- Now others are scheduled to receive God's mercy in the same way the Gentiles did.
- Everyone has been in unbelief, and everyone will have a chance to experience God's great mercy.
- There is nothing like the wisdom of God—it is beyond our comprehension. God's wisdom, knowledge, judgments, and ways are infinite.
- God's counsels are not with men—they are hidden in His person from eternity past.
- He owes us nothing; He gives us everything.

I will allow Romans 11:36, the last verse in this chapter, to speak for itself: *"For of him, and through him, and to him, are all things: to whom be glory for ever. Amen."*

Paul made his argument against replacement theology in a way that was both straightforward and succinct. There is no greater truth than the truth recorded in God's Word.

Replacement theology is a lie, and God's Word is the truth—our ultimate authority. We can be confident in placing our trust in what the Word of God says about the relationship between God and His chosen people, the Jews. He has not forsaken them, and He will not forsake them. For this reason, we can rest assured that He will never forsake those who have put their trust in Him!

APPENDIX A

HOLD THE LINE!

What can we do as individual believers to withstand the insidious effects of replacement theology?

First, we can obey the Word of God and pray for the peace of Jerusalem. Psalm 122:6 says: *"Pray for the peace of Jerusalem: they shall prosper that love thee."*

God chose to place His name there, and He has also chosen it as His capital forever. The administrative headquarters of the Godhead in eternity will be the New Jerusalem.

I have visited the earthly Jerusalem, and it is a beautiful city, but it is not at peace. There is tension in the very atmosphere. Let us pray for its peace, not just the absence of outward conflict, but peace in its inhabitants' hearts with God and with one another.

Second, we can support Israel-focused missions. Israel needs and welcomes our assistance. (When you give to Revival Nation, you are helping with our missions work in Israel.)

Continue to advocate for Israel and the Jewish people at every opportunity. This does not mean that what Israel or the Jews do is always right. Nations and individuals all make mistakes, and sometimes those mistakes have costly consequences.

Nevertheless, Israel has just as much right to exist as any other nation, and the Jews are just as legitimate a people, and just as much loved by God as any other people group.

Third, we can reject replacement theology consistently and firmly. We can reject antisemitism thoroughly in all of its forms, whenever and wherever it may arise.

The information in this book gives you principles and tools to enable you to do that.

Continue to read and study the Bible, and become familiar with it. Without a thorough understanding of true doctrine, we are in danger of falling victim to false doctrine.

Keep in mind that whatever you may be hearing about replacement theology is not new—it is centuries old, and it is just as wrong now as when it began.

> **And the peace of God, which passeth all understanding, shall keep your hearts and minds through Christ Jesus (Philippians 4:7).**

APPENDIX B

DEBUNKING REPLACEMENT THEOLOGY

What does the Bible say about Israel's future?

The following Scriptures confirm God's continuing relationship with the nation of Israel.

GENESIS 12:1-3

Now the Lord had said unto Abram, Get thee out of thy country, and from thy kindred, and from thy father's house, unto a land that I will shew thee: And I will make of thee a great nation, and I will bless thee, and make thy name great; and thou shalt be a blessing: And I will bless them that bless thee, and curse him that curseth thee: and in thee shall all families of the earth be blessed.

GENESIS 13:15-17

For all the land which thou seest, to thee will I give it, and to thy seed for ever. And I will make thy seed as the dust of the earth: so that if a man can number the dust of the earth, then shall thy seed also be numbered. Arise, walk through the land in the length of it and in the breadth of it; for I will give it unto thee.

GENESIS 17:7-8

And I will establish my covenant between me and thee and thy seed after thee in their generations for an everlasting covenant, to be a God unto thee, and to thy seed after thee. And I will give unto thee, and to thy seed after thee, the land wherein thou art a stranger, all the land of Canaan, for an everlasting possession; and I will be their God.

GENESIS 18:17-18

And the Lord said, Shall I hide from Abraham that thing which I do; Seeing that Abraham shall surely become a great and mighty nation, and all the nations of the earth shall be blessed in him?

GENESIS 22:18

And in thy seed shall all the nations of the earth be blessed; because thou hast obeyed my voice.

EXODUS 19:3-6

And Moses went up unto God, and the Lord called unto him out of the mountain, saying, Thus shalt thou say to the house of Jacob, and tell the children of Israel; ye have seen what I did unto the Egyptians, and how I bare you on eagles' wings, and brought you unto myself. Now therefore, if ye will obey my voice indeed, and keep my covenant, then ye shall be a peculiar treasure unto me above all people: for all the earth is mine: And ye shall be unto me a kingdom of priests, and an holy nation. These are the words which thou shalt speak unto the children of Israel.

LEVITICUS 26:44–45

And yet for all that, when they be in the land of their enemies, I will not cast them away, neither will I abhor them, to destroy them utterly, and to break my covenant with them: for I am the Lord their God. But I will for their sakes remember the covenant of their ancestors, whom I brought forth out of the land of Egypt in the sight of the heathen, that I might be their God: I am the Lord.

DEUTERONOMY 7:6-10

For thou art an holy people unto the Lord thy God: the Lord thy God hath chosen thee to be a special people unto himself, above all people that are upon the face of the earth. The Lord did not set his love upon you, nor choose you, because ye were more in number than any people; for ye were the fewest of all people: But because the Lord loved you, and because he would keep the oath which he had sworn unto your fathers, hath the Lord brought you out with a mighty hand, and redeemed you out of the house of bondmen, from the hand of Pharaoh king of Egypt.

Know therefore that the Lord thy God, he is God, the faithful God, which keepeth covenant and mercy with them that love him and keep his commandments to a thousand generations; and repayeth them that hate him to their face, to destroy them: he will not be slack to him that hateth him, he will repay him to his face.

DEUTERONOMY 10:15

Only the Lord had a delight in thy fathers to love them, and he chose their seed after them, even you above all people, as it is this day.

2 SAMUEL 7:12-16

And when thy days be fulfilled, and thou shalt sleep with thy fathers, I will set up thy seed after thee, which shall proceed out of thy bowels, and I will establish his kingdom. He shall build an house for my name, and I will stablish the throne of his kingdom for ever. I will be his father, and he shall be my son. If he commit iniquity, I will chasten him with the rod of men, and with the stripes of the children of men: But my mercy shall not depart away from him, as I took it from Saul, whom I put away before thee. And thine house and thy kingdom shall be established for ever before thee: thy throne shall be established for ever.

1 CHRONICLES 16:14-22

He is the Lord our God; his judgments are in all the earth. Be ye mindful always of his covenant; the word which he commanded to a thousand generations; even of the covenant which he made with Abraham, and of his oath unto Isaac; and hath confirmed the same to Jacob for a law, and to Israel for an everlasting covenant, saying, Unto thee will I give the land of Canaan, the lot of your inheritance; when ye were but few, even a few, and strangers in it. And when they went from nation to nation, and from one kingdom to another people; he suffered no man to do them wrong: yea, he reproved kings for their sakes, Saying, Touch not mine anointed, and do my prophets no harm.

PSALM 89:34-36

My covenant will I not break, nor alter the thing that is gone out of my lips. Once have I sworn by my holiness that I will not lie unto David. His seed shall endure for ever, and his throne as the sun before me.

PSALM 105:8-15

He hath remembered his covenant for ever, the word which he commanded to a thousand generations. Which covenant he made with Abraham, and his oath unto Isaac; and confirmed the same unto Jacob for a law, and to Israel for an everlasting covenant: Saying, Unto thee will I give the land of Canaan, the lot of your inheritance: When they were but a few men in number; yea, very few, and strangers in it. When they went from one nation to another, from one kingdom to another people; he suffered no man to do them wrong: yea, he reproved kings for their sakes; saying, Touch not mine anointed, and do my prophets no harm.

ISAIAH 9:6-7

For unto us a child is born, unto us a son is given: and the government shall be upon his shoulder: and his name shall be called Wonderful, Counsellor, The mighty God, The everlasting Father, The Prince of Peace. Of the increase of his government and peace there shall be no end, upon the throne of David, and upon his kingdom, to order it, and to establish it with judgment and with justice from henceforth even for ever. The zeal of the Lord of hosts will perform this.

ISAIAH 49:14-18

But Zion said, The Lord hath forsaken me, and my Lord hath forgotten me. Can a woman forget her sucking child, that she should not have compassion on the son of her womb? yea, they may forget, yet will I not forget thee. Behold, I have graven thee upon the palms of my hands; thy walls are continually before me. Thy children shall make haste; thy destroyers and they that made thee waste shall go forth of thee. Lift up thine eyes round about, and behold: all these gather themselves together, and come to thee. As I live, saith the Lord, thou shalt surely clothe thee with them all, as with an ornament, and bind them on thee, as a bride doeth.

ISAIAH 61:1-9

The Spirit of the Lord God is upon me; because the Lord hath anointed me to preach good tidings unto the meek; he hath sent me to bind up the broken-hearted, to proclaim liberty to the captives, and the opening of the prison to them that are bound; to proclaim the acceptable year of the Lord, and the day of vengeance of our God; to comfort all that mourn; to appoint unto them that mourn in Zion, to give unto them beauty for ashes, the oil of joy for mourning, the garment of praise for the spirit of heaviness; that they might be called trees of righteousness, the planting of the Lord, that he might be glorified. And they shall build the old wastes, they shall raise up the former desolations, and they shall repair the waste cities, the desolations of many generations. And strangers shall stand and feed your flocks, and the sons of the alien shall be your plowmen and your vinedressers. But ye shall be named the Priests of the Lord: men shall call you the Ministers of our God: ye shall eat the riches of the Gentiles, and in their glory shall ye boast yourselves. For your shame ye shall have double; and for confusion they shall rejoice in their portion: therefore in their land they shall possess the double: everlasting joy shall be unto them. For I the Lord love judgment, I hate robbery for burnt offering; and I will direct their work in truth, and I will make an everlasting covenant with them. And their seed shall be known among the Gentiles, and their offspring among the people: all that see them shall acknowledge them, that they are the seed which the Lord hath blessed.

JEREMIAH 31:31-37

Behold, the days come, saith the Lord, that I will make a new covenant with the house of Israel, and with the house of Judah: Not according to the covenant that I made with their fathers in the day that I took them by the hand to bring them out of the land of Egypt; which my covenant they brake, although I was an husband unto them, saith the Lord: But this shall be the covenant that I will make with the house of Israel; After those days, saith the Lord, I will put my law in their inward parts, and write it in their hearts; and will be their God, and they shall be my people. And they shall teach no more every man his neighbour, and every man his brother, saying, Know the Lord: for they shall all know me, from the least of them unto the greatest of them, saith the Lord: for I will forgive their iniquity, and I will remember their sin no more. Thus saith the Lord, which giveth the sun for a light by day, and the ordinances of the moon and of the stars for a light by night, which divideth the sea when the waves thereof roar; The Lord of hosts is his name: If those ordinances depart from before me, saith the Lord, then the seed of Israel also shall cease from being a nation before me for ever. Thus saith the Lord; If heaven above can be measured, and the foundations of the earth searched out beneath, I will also cast off all the seed of Israel for all that they have done, saith the Lord.

EZEKIEL 36:22-28

Therefore say unto the house of Israel, thus saith the Lord God; I do not this for your sakes, O house of Israel, but for mine holy name's sake, which ye have profaned among the heathen, whither ye went. And I will sanctify my great name, which was profaned among the heathen, which ye have profaned in the midst of them; and the heathen shall know that I am the Lord, saith the Lord God, when I shall be sanctified in you before their eyes. For I will take you from among the heathen, and gather you out of all countries, and will bring you into your own land. Then will I sprinkle clean water upon you, and ye shall be clean: from all your filthiness, and from all your idols, will I cleanse you. A new heart also will I give you, and a new spirit will I put within you: and I will take away the stony heart out of your flesh, and I will give you an heart of flesh. And I will put my spirit within you, and cause you to walk in my statutes, and ye shall keep my judgments, and do them. And ye shall dwell in the land that I gave to your fathers; and ye shall be my people, and I will be your God.

EZEKIEL 36:35-36

And they shall say, This land that was desolate is become like the garden of Eden; and the waste and desolate and ruined cities are become fenced, and are inhabited. Then the heathen that are left round about you shall know that I the Lord build the ruined places, and plant that that was desolate: I the Lord have spoken it, and I will do it.

EZEKIEL 37:11-14

Then he said unto me, Son of man, these bones are the whole house of Israel: behold, they say, Our bones are dried, and our hope is lost: we are cut off for our parts. Therefore prophesy and say unto them, Thus saith the Lord God; Behold, O my people, I will open your graves, and cause you to come up out of your graves, and bring you into the land of Israel. And ye shall know that I am the Lord, when I have opened your graves, O my people, and brought you up out of your graves, and shall put my spirit in you, and ye shall live, and I shall place you in your own land: then shall ye know that I the Lord have spoken it, and performed it, saith the Lord.

EZEKIEL 38:16

And thou shalt come up against my people of Israel, as a cloud to cover the land; it shall be in the latter days, and I will bring thee against my land, that the heathen may know me, when I shall be sanctified in thee, O Gog, before their eyes.

HOSEA 14:4-7

I will heal their backsliding, I will love them freely: for mine anger is turned away from him. I will be as the dew unto Israel: he shall grow as the lily, and cast forth his roots as Lebanon. His branches shall spread, and his beauty shall be as the olive tree, and his smell as Lebanon. They that dwell under his shadow shall return; they shall revive as the corn, and grow as the vine: the scent thereof shall be as the wine of Lebanon.

AMOS 9:14-15

And I will bring again the captivity of my people of Israel, and they shall build the waste cities, and inhabit them; and they shall plant vineyards, and drink the wine thereof; they shall also make gardens, and eat the fruit of them. And I will plant them upon their land, and they shall no more be pulled up out of their land which I have given them, saith the Lord thy God.

ROMANS 4:16

Therefore it is of faith, that it might be by grace; to the end the promise might be sure to all the seed; not to that only which is of the law, but to that also which is of the faith of Abraham; who is the father of us all,

ROMANS 8:35-39

Who shall separate us from the love of Christ? shall tribulation, or distress, or persecution, or famine, or nakedness, or peril, or sword? As it is written, For thy sake we are killed all the day long; we are accounted as sheep for the slaughter. Nay, in all these things we are more than conquerors through him that loved us. For I am persuaded, that neither death, nor life, nor angels, nor principalities, nor powers, nor things present, nor things to come, nor height, nor depth, nor any other creature, shall be able to separate us from the love of God, which is in Christ Jesus our Lord.

ROMANS 9:1-5

I say the truth in Christ, I lie not, my conscience also bearing me witness in the Holy Ghost, that I have great heaviness and continual sorrow in my heart. For I could wish that myself were accursed from Christ for my brethren, my kinsmen according to the flesh: Who are Israelites; to whom pertaineth the adoption, and the glory, and the covenants, and the giving of the law, and the service of God, and the promises; whose are the fathers, and of whom as concerning the flesh

Christ came, who is over all, God blessed for ever. Amen.

ROMANS 11:1-36

I say then, Hath God cast away his people? God forbid. For I also am an Israelite, of the seed of Abraham, of the tribe of Benjamin. God hath not cast away his people which he foreknew. Wot ye not what the scripture saith of Elias? how he maketh intercession to God against Israel saying, Lord, they have killed thy prophets, and digged down thine altars; and I am left alone, and they seek my life. But what saith the answer of God unto him? I have reserved to myself seven thousand men, who have not bowed the knee to the image of Baal. Even so then at this present time also there is a remnant according to the election of grace. And if by grace, then is it no more of works: otherwise grace is no more grace.

But if it be of works, then it is no more grace: otherwise work is no more work. What then? Israel hath not obtained that which he seeketh for; but the election hath obtained it, and the rest were blinded. (According as it is written, God hath given them the spirit of slumber, eyes that they should not see, and ears that they should not hear;) unto this day. And David saith, Let their table be made a snare, and a trap, and a stumbling block, and a recompence unto them: Let their eyes be darkened, that they may not see, and bow down their back alway. I say then, Have they stumbled that they should fall? God forbid: but rather through their fall salvation is come unto the Gentiles, for to provoke them to jealousy. Now if the fall of them be the riches of the world, and the diminishing of them the riches of the Gentiles; how much more their fulness?

For I speak to you Gentiles, inasmuch as I am the apostle of the Gentiles, I magnify mine office: If by any means I may provoke to emulation them which are my flesh, and might save some of them. For if the casting away of them be the reconciling of the world, what shall the receiving of them be, but life from the dead? For if the firstfruit be holy, the lump is also holy: and if the root be holy, so are the branches. And if some of the branches be broken off, and thou, being a wild olive tree, wert grafted in among them, and with them partakest of the root and fatness of the olive tree; boast not against the branches. But if thou boast, thou bearest not the root, but the root thee. Thou wilt say then, The branches were broken off, that I might be grafted in. Well; because of unbelief they were broken off, and thou standest by faith.

Be not highminded, but fear: For if God spared not the natural branches, take heed lest he also spare not thee. Behold therefore the goodness and severity of God: on them which fell, severity; but toward thee, goodness, if thou continue in his goodness: otherwise thou also shalt be cut off. And they also, if they abide not still in unbelief, shall be grafted in: for God is able to graft them in again. For if thou wert cut out of the olive tree which is wild by nature, and wert grafted contrary to nature into a good olive tree: how much more shall these, which be the natural branches, be grafted into their own olive tree? For I would not, brethren, that ye should be ignorant of this mystery, lest ye should be wise in your own conceits; that blindness in part is happened to Israel, until the fulness of the Gentiles be come in. And so all Israel shall be saved: as it is written, There shall come out of Sion the Deliverer, and shall turn away ungodliness from Jacob: For this is my covenant unto them, when I shall take away their sins.

As concerning the gospel, they are enemies for your sakes: but as touching the election, they are beloved for the father's sakes. For the gifts and calling of God are without repentance. For as ye in times past have not believed God, yet have now obtained mercy through their unbelief: Even so have these also now not believed, that through your mercy they also may obtain mercy. For God hath concluded them all in unbelief, that he might have mercy upon all. O the depth of the riches both of the wisdom and knowledge of God! how unsearchable are his judgments, and his ways past finding out! For who hath known the mind of the Lord? or who hath been his counsellor? Or who hath first given to him, and it shall be recompensed unto him again? For of him, and through him, and to him, are all things: to whom be glory for ever. Amen.

REVELATION 7:3-4

Saying, Hurt not the earth, neither the sea, nor the trees, till we have sealed the servants of our God in their foreheads. And I heard the number of them which were sealed: and there were sealed an hundred and forty and four thousand of all the tribes of the children of Israel.

REVELATION 12:1-6

And there appeared a great wonder in heaven; a woman clothed with the sun, and the moon under her feet, and upon her head a crown of twelve stars: And she being with child cried, travailing in birth, and pained to be delivered. And there appeared another wonder in heaven; and behold a great red dragon, having seven heads and ten horns, and seven crowns upon his heads. And his tail drew the third part of the stars of heaven, and did cast them to the earth: and the dragon stood before the woman which was ready to be delivered, for to devour her child as soon as it was born. And she brought forth a man child, who was to rule all nations with a rod of iron: and her child was caught up unto God, and to his throne. And the woman fled into the wilderness, where she hath a place prepared of God, that they should feed her there a thousand two hundred and threescore days.

REVELATION 12:13-17

And when the dragon saw that he was cast unto the earth, he persecuted the woman which brought forth the man child. And to the woman were given two wings of a great eagle, that she might fly into the wilderness, into her place, where she is nourished for a time, and times, and half a time, from the face of the serpent. And the serpent cast out of his mouth water as a flood after the woman, that he might cause her to be carried away of the flood. And the earth helped the woman, and the earth opened her mouth, and swallowed up the flood which the dragon cast out of his mouth. And the dragon was wroth with the woman, and went to make war with the remnant of her seed, which keep the commandments of God, and have the testimony of Jesus Christ.

APPENDIX C

ISRAEL AND REVIVAL

A 20th Century Timeline

Throughout the 20th century, moments of prophetic significance in Israel often unfolded alongside seasons of spiritual awakening in the United States. While correlation does not prove causation, the historical record reveals a striking pattern. As Israel moved closer to covenant fulfillment, the Church in the United States frequently experienced revival.

This Appendix simply lays history side by side. When Israel stepped into pivotal moments, revival fires often burned hotter in America. For those who take Scripture seriously, especially the promises concerning Israel's restoration, these parallel movements deserve thoughtful consideration.

1906 TO 1915

Israel: Zionist movement gains momentum toward a Jewish homeland.

America: Azusa Street Revival begins in 1906, launching modern Pentecostalism and global Spirit-filled missions.

1914 TO 1917

Israel: World War I reshapes the Middle East. Balfour Declaration issued in 1917 supporting a Jewish national home.

America: Pentecostal movement organizes nationally. Assemblies of God founded in 1914.

1947

Israel: United Nations adopts the Partition Plan for Palestine.

America: Post-war Healing Revival surges across the nation with mass tent meetings.

1948

Israel: State of Israel declared May 14, 1948.

America: Healing Revivals intensify. Latter Rain movement begins, emphasizing restoration themes.

1967

Israel: Six-Day War. Jerusalem comes under Jewish control.

America: Charismatic Renewal accelerates. Momentum builds toward the Jesus Movement.

LATE 1960S TO EARLY 1970S

Israel: Global focus on Jerusalem increases after 1967.

America: Jesus Movement spreads nationwide. Asbury Revival breaks out in 1970.

1973

Israel: Yom Kippur War shocks the nation.

America: Jesus Movement and Charismatic Renewal remain strong with mass evangelism and the Word of Faith Renewal begins to spread.

1978

Israel: Camp David Accords signed.

America: Charismatic and Word of Faith movements mature and expand influence across denominations. The Moral Majority is founded and begins to effect national elections.

1994 TO 1995

Israel: Rabin assassination marks a national turning point.

America: Toronto Blessing begins in 1994. Brownsville Revival begins in 1995.

As you step back from the dates and headlines, a pattern emerges that is difficult to ignore. When Israel moved through moments of covenant significance, the American Church often moved through moments of spiritual intensity. The rebirth of a nation, wars over Jerusalem, political turning points, each seem to echo with seasons of repentance, renewal, and revival on our shores.

This does not mean America replaces Israel, and it does not mean revival depends on geopolitics. It means God's redemptive purposes are not random. He keeps covenant with Israel, and He awakens His Church in prophetic times.

For those who believe that Scripture governs history, these parallel movements serve as both a reminder and a warning. Watch Israel. Watch the Church. And above all, be ready. Jesus is coming.

Maranatha!

ABOUT ALAN DIDIO

Pastor Alan DiDio is the host of *Revival Nation* and the founder of Revival Nation Church. In more than two decades of ministry, he has traveled internationally working with the persecuted Church around the world and directed an international prayer center where he prayed one-on-one with more than 100,000 people. This unique experience comes out in his writings and ministry as he seeks to ignite the fire of God in the hearts of humanity and equip end-time believers for the next great awakening.

Alan DiDio was an avowed atheist—that is until he had a transforming, radical encounter with the living God at age 17. After giving his life to Christ, Pastor Alan attended a Christian college and began working with an international ministry, where he gained experience in every possible area of ministry from running a prayer center to traveling across the country spreading the gospel.

He has since launched Encounter Ministries with the new emphasis and branding of Revival Nation.

To connect with Pastor Alan, visit: www.RevivalNation.com

From

Alan DiDio

Confront Satan's End-Time Deceptions Head-On!

In this era of unparalleled technological advances, artificial intelligence reshapes our world and UFOs are found daily in the headlines. Believers are faced with urgent, soul-stirring questions: Is there a trace of AI in biblical prophecy? Could the antichrist manipulate this technology to dominate our era? Does the Bible talk about aliens? Above all, how should the Church, armed with ancient wisdom, respond to this modern revolution?

Asking these same questions, Alan DiDio, a formidable apostolic and prophetic leader and the dynamic force behind the Encounter Today YouTube channel, embarked on a quest for truth. Through extensive research and revelatory interviews, he brings to light a balanced narrative, juxtaposing the potential of AI against the unchanging truths of biblical prophecies and the unfolding of global events.

Armed with this prophetic insight, you are called to rise, unshakable in your crucial end-time role. It's time to seize your destiny and light the way in this revolutionary age!

Purchase your copy wherever books are sold.

In the Right Hands, This Book Will Change Lives!

Most of the people who need this message will not be looking for this book. To change their lives, you need to **put a copy of this book in their hands.**

Our ministry is constantly seeking methods to find the people who need this anointed message to change their lives. **Will you help us reach these people?**

Extend this ministry by sowing three, five, ten, or *even more* books today and change people's lives for the better! Your generosity will be part of catalyzing the Great Awakening that many have been prophesying and praying for.